ETF Fundamentals

azLearning Publishing

Published by azLearning Publishing, 2024.

While every precaution has been taken in the preparation of this book, the publisher assumes no responsibility for errors or omissions, or for damages resulting from the use of the information contained herein.

ETF FUNDAMENTALS

First edition. September 13, 2024.

ISBN: 979-8224824007

Written by azLearning Publishing.

Table of Contents

For dedicated and motivated investors throughout the world!

Acknowledgements

Book cover photograph by

Martin Ceralde

@martinceralde

Free to use under the Unsplash License

Book cover design by

Eric Jakows

@ericjakows

General Disclaimers

This book is intended for educational purposes only. The information provided is not a substitute for professional financial advice. Consult a qualified financial advisor before making any investment decisions.

The information contained in this book is believed to be accurate as of the publication date. However, the author and publisher make no representations or warranties regarding the completeness or accuracy of the content, and will not be held liable for any errors, omissions, or changes in the information provided.

This book references information from third-party sources. The author and publisher are not responsible for the accuracy or reliability of any third-party information.

The author and publisher disclaim any liability for losses or damages incurred by readers as a result of their reliance on information or strategies discussed in this book.

Financial Disclaimers

This book does not constitute an offer to sell or the solicitation of an offer to buy any securities, investment products, or financial instruments.

Investing in financial markets involves risk, including the potential loss of principal. Certain investments, such as ETFs, options, and derivatives, may carry additional risks. Please assess your risk tolerance before making any investments.

Past performance is not indicative of future results. The strategies discussed in this book do not guarantee specific outcomes, and all investments carry risks, including the loss of principal.

The author may hold positions in securities or other financial instruments mentioned in this book. Any mention of specific securities or financial instruments is not a recommendation or endorsement by the author.

This publication is not endorsed by, nor does it represent the views of, the Securities and Exchange Commission or any other regulatory body.

This book may contain forward-looking statements, which are subject to risks and uncertainties. Actual results may differ materially from those projected in any forward-looking statements.

This book does not provide tax advice. Tax laws and regulations are complex and subject to change. Please consult a qualified tax advisor to understand the tax implications of any investment strategies discussed in this book.

Chapter 1: Welcome to ETFs

How do exchange-traded funds work? Exchange-traded funds (ETFs) are investment funds that trade on stock exchanges, similar to stocks. They are investment vehicles that mimic stock market trading and are known as exchange-traded funds (ETFs). They hold a basket of securities in their fund. In order to keep the price of their holdings, which can include equities, commodities, or bonds, relatively near to the fund's net asset value (NAV), these investors often use arbitrage tactics. Investments in exchange-traded funds (ETFs) provide diversification, cost savings, and tax benefits to their owners. ETFs, in contrast to mutual funds, are tradable at any moment during the trading day at the current market price.

There are a lot of benefits to exchange-traded funds, and investors should find out more about them. Many investors are already familiar with mutual funds due to their long history. Buying and selling of mutual funds occurs at the end of each trading day, with prices determined by the closing net asset value (NAV). Conversely, exchange-traded funds (ETFs) offer intraday trading flexibility, which is a crucial benefit of funds during periods of excessive volatility since it allows investors to react quickly to market changes. One major benefit over mutual funds is the instantaneous market liquidity this provides to your investment account.

This book provides a thorough introduction to exchange-traded funds (ETFs) and will be helpful for investors of all experience levels. Also included is a review of the following well-known and significant ETFs:

$SPY (SPDR S&P 500 ETF Trust)

$QQQ (Invesco QQQ Trust)

$IWM (iShares Russell 2000 ETF)

$EWZ (iShares MSCI Brazil ETF)

$SLV (iShares Silver Trust)

You, the Investor:

What type of investor are you?

We will touch on this topic briefly but not go into great detail. In addition to understanding the financial markets, investors need to understand themselves. Do you consider yourself to be an investor or a trader? Are you a day trader or a scalper? (Depending on the situation, you can be a combination.) What is your time horizon for making money? It can be days, months, or years. ETFs can be invested in for a variety of objectives, goals, and time horizons. ETFs can be used to achieve a wide range of investing objectives, such as growth or income. For focused and serious investors exchange-traded funds can build wealth and help achieve many goals. It's important that you understand both your personality and investing style. Here, a plethora of concerns and queries are raised. What are the dollar and percentage return targets do you have set for your investments? How much (quantifiable) risk are you willing to take? Whether you invest in exchange-traded funds (ETFs) or any other kind of investment, you should always do an investor self-examination. One of the reasons FINRA and the SEC require investment firms to know their customer is all about knowing your investment makeup. The psychology of individual investors is very important. Investment firms create a know-your-customer profile for their clients that is both for regulatory compliance purposes and is mutually beneficial.

Globally, ETF assets under management (AUM) have surpassed $9 trillion, a sign of the industry's success in this area of finance. One example is the SPDR S&P 500 ETF Trust, which is responsible for over $560 billion in assets. U.S. stock market trading volume in dollars was 32% attributable to ETF trading.

This growth highlights the opportunities accessible to investors now and the prevalence of exchange-traded funds (ETFs), which did not exist thirty-some years ago. The question of whether exchange-traded funds (ETFs) are a good fit for your investing strategy should be based on your individual goals and circumstances. Given the multitude of factors that depend on you, your goals, and other personal circumstances, a definitive answer is not possible. In today's expansive and varied world of exchange-traded fund investing, there are investment opportunities for everyone. Simple exchange-traded funds based on market capitalization weights aren't your only option.

Beyond simple index funds, investors can pick from a wide range of ETFs. Some of the most common kinds are these:

Equity ETFs: They track companies or stock indexes based on market caps (small-cap, large-cap), industry sectors (technology, healthcare, etc.), or both.

Bond/Fixed-Income ETFs: These focus on bonds and other fixed-income securities, providing exposure to government, corporate, or municipal bonds.

Commodity ETFs: These ETFs invest in physical commodities like gold, silver, oil, or agricultural products. Most commodity ETFs own the physical commodity. The SPDR Gold **Shares ETF (GLD)** owns about 27 million ounces in its various vaults and has an expense ratio of 0.4%.

Currency ETFs: These track the performance of foreign currencies, allowing investors to gain exposure to currency fluctuations.

Real Estate ETFs: These invest in real estate investment trusts (REITs) or real estate-related indexes.

Sector and Industry ETFs: These focus on specific sectors or industries, such as technology, healthcare, or energy.

Thematic ETFs: These target specific investment themes or trends, such as clean energy, robotics, or artificial intelligence.

Inverse and Leveraged ETFs: These are designed to provide the opposite performance of an index (inverse) or amplify an index's returns (leveraged). These ETFs are for aggressive and sophisticated investors who actively manage their accounts daily.

Sustainable/ESG ETFs: These focus on companies that meet specific environmental, social, and governance (ESG) criteria.

Multi-Asset ETFs: These invest in a mix of asset classes, such as stocks, bonds, and commodities, to provide diversified exposure.

Notice: This book provides general information and is not intended to offer specific investment recommendations or taxation advice. Before making any financial decisions, always get advice from a qualified professional specialist. The ETFs that are described in this book are merely examples and are not meant to be taken as investment advice.

Chapter 2: ETFS's Origins

A Look at the Evolution of ETFs

Launched in 1993, the SPDR S&P 500 ETF Trust (SPY) was the initial US-based ETF to achieve significant success. Growth was slow at first since not enough institutions were using ETFs, but that all changed in the late 1990s when investors began to see the value of ETFs. The exponentially expanding exchange-traded fund (ETF) market has since grown to encompass almost every investment method, industry, and asset class imaginable. Among the most recent developments is the proliferation of inverse, leveraged, and theme exchange-traded funds (ETFs), which have increased market diversity.

A common theme in the financial media is the rapid expansion of ETFs. Most proponents of low-cost index funds have enthusiastically embraced these well-liked funds, whose assets have more than doubled annually since 1995 (as of 2001). Among index funds, Vanguard is the most vocal proponent.

In the year 2000, the initial European exchange-traded fund (ETF) was introduced to the public. In 2006, ProShares unveiled the first leveraged exchange-traded fund (ETF). U.S. exchange-traded funds (ETFs) managed $2 trillion in assets in December 2014.

Bitwise Asset Management, ProShares, and VanEck were the first to provide exchange-traded funds (ETFs) pegged to the price of cryptocurrency Ethereum in October 2023.

With 34% of market share BlackRock, Vanguard (29%), State Street (14%), Invesco, and Charles Schwab are currently the top exchange-traded fund (ETF) issuers. More and more businesses are using ETFs for fund management and other investment-related activities.

Mutual fund shares are overseen by governmental agencies, such the SEC and CFTC in the US.

BlackRock, Vanguard, and State Street have been instrumental in the development and expansion of the ETF industry.

> **BlackRock** has been at the forefront of ETF innovation, offering specialized products such as ESG (Environmental, Social, and Governance) ETFs, factor-based ETFs (like Smart Beta), and thematic ETFs. These products cater to both institutional and retail investors, providing tools to meet diverse investment needs.

> **Vanguard** offers a wide range of ETFs, with a strong focus on broad-based index funds. These ETFs provide exposure to large segments of the market, such as the total U.S. stock market, international markets, and various bond indices.

> **State Street** is a leader in offering sector-specific ETFs through its SPDR series. These ETFs allow investors to target specific sectors of the economy, such as technology, healthcare, or financials, providing tools for both tactical investing and sector rotation strategies.

Around seventy to seventy-five percent of all exchange-traded fund assets (ETF AUM) are located in the United States, making it the world's leading investor in ETFs. Europe is home to around 15-20% of the world's exchange-traded fund assets, making it the second-largest market for these funds.

Chapter 3: Recent Trends

Innovations in the ETF Space:

The ETF market continues to grow with innovations such as Smart Beta ETFs, which combine passive indexing with active management strategies to offer investors more tailored exposure.

Thematic ETFs are also gaining popularity. They allow investors to focus on specific industries, trends, or economic themes, such as clean energy or artificial intelligence.

ESG ETFs: Environmental, Social, and Governance (ESG) ETFs are also becoming more prominent, catering to investors who prioritize ethical investing.

Crypto ETFs: Some of the most notable cryptocurrency ETFs are those that track the performance of Bitcoin and Ethereum, the two largest cryptocurrencies by market capitalization. These ETFs either hold the actual cryptocurrency (physical ETFs) or track futures contracts or other financial instruments that derive their value from the cryptocurrency (futures-based ETFs). With Bitcoin at about the $60,000 level as of this writing, demand for all-things crypto remains strong.

Investors poured $122 billion into U.S. exchange-traded funds in July 2024. That was the second-highest monthly total on record, behind $128 billion in December 2023, and the fourth month with inflows north of $100 billion. These are considerable investment inflows into the ETF marketplace.

Once again, ETFs globally are now over $9 trillion in total market size. Much of this immense growth is related to the current bull market investors have experienced over the past fifteen years or so. It will be interesting to see what happens to the ETF marketplace during a market correction or a prolonged market downturn. The ability to quickly liquidate ETFs and also to change asset allocations with sector rotation strategies has been a major selling point emphasized to investors. Whether or not ETF investors will adapt to bearish market conditions with prudent asset allocation strategies will be an interesting development to examine. ETF investors consists of both institutional and individual retail investors. No matter who you are and no matter the size of your investment holdings, closely monitoring the ETF marketplace will be always the smart thing to do.

Chapter 4: ETFs vs. Mutual Funds

ETFs and mutual funds share several commonalities. Both offer a wide variety of investment choices, they are professionally managed, and also they help investors achieve diversification.

Structure and Trading: ETFs and mutual funds both offer pooled investments in a diversified portfolio with specific fund objectives. However, while mutual funds are priced once at the end of the trading day, ETFs are traded on stock exchanges and shares are priced throughout the day during regular trading hours.

With ETFs trading on a stock exchange daily they can also be sold short using borrowed funds from a stockbroker (using a margin account). Additionally, ETFs can be bought and sold using limit orders just as common stock investors use limit orders.

ETFs also enjoy lower investment minimums. One single share of an ETF is typically the minimum investment and even less if the brokerage allows for owning fractional shares. Whereas, a mutual fund may require a $1000, $3000 or more to begin.

Tax Efficiency: Due to their structure, ETFs are generally tax-efficient, but it's important to understand how capital gains distributions work. ETFs with high turnover or specific strategies might distribute more capital gains. ETFs' unique "in-kind" creation and redemption process allows them to minimize capital gains distributions.

Expenses: Generally speaking, ETFs have lower expense ratios than mutual funds because of their passive management approach. According to Morningstar (December 2023) the average expense ratio for ETFs is 0.57% and for mutual funds 0.85%. With compounding, over time, that becomes significant.

Vanguard is now a trailblazer in the ETF space and is well-known for its inexpensive index ETFs. It is the nation's second-biggest supplier of ETFs. Fees on mutual funds are usually greater, especially if they are actively managed.

The founder of the Vanguard Group, John Bogle, was a pioneer of index funds. He was initially skeptical about ETFs in the early days and called them a "wolf in sheep's clothing." Bogle felt that the immediate liquidity of ETFs would encourage speculation and investors to chase market fads. John Bogle was right about many things, but wrong about ETFs overall.

Investors worldwide have driven the strong growth of ETFs over recent years since they have recognized that it offers the best of both worlds. A diversfied portfolio like a mutual fund and the ability and flexibility to trade the fund like a share of common stock.

Chapter 5: ETFs and Taxation

All investors share a common characteristic of desiring to keep more of what they earn. ETFs typically offer superior tax efficiency due to their unique structure. Transaction costs and management fees are minimized due to this ETF structure. Reduced ETF portfolio turnover generally results in lower expenses and lower capital gains taxes.

By comparison, in the United States, whenever a mutual fund realizes and declares a capital gain, all of its shareholders who hold the fund in taxable accounts pay a capital gains tax on their individual share of the gain. Individual investors have no control over how much capital gain a mutual fund declares at any given time.

In-kind Redemption: ETFs typically allow investors to redeem their shares by exchanging them for underlying securities, rather than selling the shares and receiving cash. This in-kind redemption process can help minimize capital gains taxes, as gains are often deferred until the underlying securities are sold.

Lower Portfolio Turnover: ETFs often have lower portfolio turnover than mutual funds, meaning they less frequently buy and sell securities. This reduced turnover can lead to lower transaction costs and fewer capital gains realizations, which can result in lower overall tax burdens.

Tax-Loss Harvesting: Strategies can be employed to use ETFs for tax-loss harvesting. You can sell losing ETFs to offset gains and reduce tax liability (Tax-Loss Harvesting). Be aware of the "wash sale" rule, which prevents repurchasing the same or substantially identical security within 30 days.

Wash Sale Rule: It's important to be aware of the wash sale rule, which prohibits the repurchase of the same or substantially identical security within 30 days of selling it at a loss. This rule is designed to prevent investors from artificially creating losses for tax purposes.

Individual Circumstances: Tax laws can change over time, and individual circumstances (e.g., income level, investment goals) can significantly impact tax strategies. It's essential to consult with a tax professional to determine the most appropriate approach for your specific situation.

Long-Term vs. Short-Term Gains: The tax treatment of capital gains depends on whether they are short-term (held for less than one year) or long-term (held for one year or more). Long-term gains generally have lower tax rates than short-term gains. These tax rates vary considerably across countries.

In a regular taxable brokerage account, yes you pay taxes on the gains you make from selling shares. You can buy and sell whatever you want with no immediate tax consequences in an IRA or another tax advantaged account.

A great feature of ETFs and capital gains taxes is that you can control the timing of when you sell and realize your gain. If you currently have a good gain with your ETF fund(s) you can choose to sell this year, next year or five years from now depending upon your investment and tax circumstances and strategies. ETF shareholders call the shots as to when they sell their shares. If you own a mutual fund, they decide when capital gains are declared. If you own a municipal bond, it can be called away when interest rates fall. The flexibility of controlling when you sell your ETF shares cannot be overeremphasized.

In Europe, depending upon the country, investors experience a wide range of taxes on ETFs ranging from zero percent all the way to the low forties. Greece and Bulgaria are among the lowest countries for taxing ETFs, while Ireland and Denmark are at the top of the list.

By understanding the tax implications of ETFs and mutual funds, investors can make more informed decisions about their investment portfolios and potentially reduce their overall tax burden.

Chapter 6: $SPY (SPDR® S&P 500® ETF Trust)

$SPY, the biggest, most liquid, and oldest U.S. exchange-traded fund, offers exposure to the S&P 500 Index, which serves as a benchmark for 500 large-cap U.S. equities. The S&P 500 is basically the gold standard for the investment world. Most ETFs are index funds. Its simplicity, liquidity, and capacity to track the performance of the larger market are the main reasons for its popularity. On January 22, 1993, more than thirty years ago, the SPY ETF was founded. Renowned for being the pioneer in the U.S. ETF market, State Street Global Advisors continues to lead, especially when it comes to sector and large-cap U.S. equities ETFs. State Street says that the SPY fund "democratized investing and set the ETF market in motion."

The shares of this ETF trust are traded on the Arca platform of the New York Stock exchange (NYSE), and its total assets are estimated to be over $560 billion in 2024. The goal of SPY's share price is to be one-tenth of the S&P 500 Stock Index. If the S&P 500 Stock Index is at 5600, for example, then SPY will be trading at approximately $560 per share. SPY options (calls and puts) are traded on the CBOE (Chicago Board Options Exchange) with daily expirations offered. Call and put options can be written or purchased on SPY and many ETFs. This feature allows investors to implement covered call strategies to generate income and for hedging purposes.

By investing in SPY, you're essentially investing in a basket of 500 stocks. This provides instant diversification, reducing your risk of significant losses due to any single company's performance. SPY aims to replicate the performance of the S&P 500. This means its price should fluctuate in line with the overall stock market. It's designed to track an index, rather than actively picking stocks. ETFs like SPY typically have lower expense ratios compared to actively managed funds. This means more of your investment goes towards buying stocks, rather than paying fees.

SPY ETF Fund Top Holdings (as of August 2024)

Apple (AAPL)

NVIDIA (NVDA)

Microsoft (MSFT)

Amazon (AMZN)

Meta Platforms, Inc. (META)

SPY ETF Fund Top Sector Breakdown (as of August 2024)

Information Technology 31.1%

Financials 13.1%

Health Care 12.1%

Communications 8.9%

Industrials 8.4%

The average daily trading volume of the SPY ETF is 50 million shares. SPY, and other market-cap-weighted ETFs tracking the whole S&P 500 Index, have strong market liquidity.

Liquidity is a major advantage of ETFs, as they can be traded throughout the day at market prices. However, not all ETFs offer the same level of liquidity. Liquidity in ETFs is often gauged by metrics like the bid-ask spread and average daily trading volume. Highly liquid ETFs, such as the SPDR S&P 500 ETF Trust, typically have narrow bid-ask spreads and high trading volumes, making them easier to buy and sell at favorable prices.

Key Technical Indicators:

For traders interested in timing their buy/sell entry price into SPY, the following technical indicators should be considered.

Moving Averages: 50-day and 200-day moving averages are crucial. A bullish signal occurs when the 50-day crosses above the 200-day (Golden Cross), while a bearish signal occurs when the 50-day cross is below the 200-day (Death Cross).

Relative Strength Index (RSI): Watch for an RSI above 70 (overbought) or below 30 (oversold). Overbought conditions signal a pullback, while oversold conditions indicate a buying opportunity.

Volume Analysis: Monitor volume spikes on price breakouts from crucial support or resistance levels. High volume on a breakout usually confirms the move.

Beyond the commonly used moving averages and RSI, here are additional indicators to consider for $SPY:

Bollinger Bands: Can be used to identify overbought and oversold conditions and potential trend reversals.

MACD (Moving Average Convergence Divergence): A momentum indicator that can signal trend changes and potential buy or sell opportunities.

Stochastic Oscillator: Another momentum indicator that measures the speed and change of price movements.

Strategies:

Trend Following: Use moving averages and MACD to follow the trend. Buy during uptrends and sell during downtrends.

Swing Trading: Identify overbought or oversold conditions using RSI and Bollinger Bands to capitalize on short-term price movements.

Mean Reversion: Enter short positions when RSI is over 70 and exit when it returns to neutral levels.

Options Strategies: Consider selling covered calls in a range-bound market or buying protective puts during market downturns.

Dividends: Investors earn a little over a 1% dividend yield from the SPY ETF. This ETF is a growth investment and clearly not a fund for income investment.

While the mentioned strategies are effective, let's explore some more nuanced approaches:

1. Sector Rotation

Given the S&P 500's diversity, sector rotation can be a valuable strategy.

Sector ETFs: Consider using sector ETFs (e.g., $XLF for financials, $XLE for energy) to identify outperforming sectors.

Sector Rotation Strategies: Implement strategies like equal-weighting, momentum-based allocation, or thematic investing.

2. Factor Investing

Factor investing focuses on factors that drive stock returns, such as value, growth, momentum, and quality.

Factor ETFs: Explore ETFs that target these factors (e.g., $IWM for small-cap value, $IGV for growth).

Factor Combination: Combine factor ETFs to create a diversified portfolio with exposure to multiple factors. Enhanced indexing is used combing active and passive portfolio management with the goal of beating the returns of an index.

3. Dividend Investing

For income-oriented investors, SPY's dividend-paying stocks can be a source of income.

Dividend-Weighted ETFs: Consider ETFs that weight stocks based on dividend yields (e.g., $VYM). WisdomTree is known for its unique approach to dividend and earnings-weighted ETFs and for offering innovative products in emerging markets and alternative asset classes.

Dividend Reinvestment: Utilize dividend reinvestment plans (DRIPs) to compound returns over time.

4. Tactical Asset Allocation

Consider using tactical asset allocation strategies to adjust allocations based on market conditions dynamically.

Market Timing: Use technical indicators or fundamental analysis to determine when to shift allocations between SPY and other asset classes (e.g., bonds, commodities).

Risk Parity: Allocate assets based on their volatility to achieve a more balanced portfolio.

Additional Considerations

Economic Indicators: Monitor macroeconomic indicators such as GDP growth, inflation, and interest rates, as they can significantly impact SPY's performance.

Geopolitical Events: Stay updated on geopolitical events that can cause market volatility and affect SPY's price.

Corporate Earnings: Monitor corporate earnings reports, as they can drive individual stock prices and, in turn, the overall market.

By combining these strategies and factors, investors can make more informed decisions when trading SPY and potentially enhance their total returns.

Other ETFs tracking the whole S&P 500 Index:

There are many other market-cap-weighted ETFs besides the SPDR S&P 500 ETF (SPY). They include:

iShares Core S&P 500 ETF (IVV)

Vanguard S&P 500 ETF (VOO)

SPDR Portfolio S&P 500 ETF (SPLG)

Invesco S&P 500 Equal Weight ETF (RSP)

IVV from iShares advertises itself as the largest low-cost S&P 500 ETF (according to Morningstar, 10/31/2023).

Chapter 7: $QQQ (Invesco QQQ Trust)

As a leading ETF tracking the Nasdaq-100 Index, $QQQ offers exposure to the 100 largest non-financial companies listed on the Nasdaq stock exchange. Invesco is a recognized leader for its innovative financial products. The QQQ fund is a tech-heavy ETF often seen as a proxy for the U.S. tech sector, with significant holdings in giants like Apple and Microsoft.

The Invesco QQQ Trust (QQQ) is not priced at exactly 1/40th of the Nasdaq-100 Index, but it is designed to track the performance of the Nasdaq-100 Index closely.

Many of the companies in the Nasdaq-100 are growth-oriented, meaning they have the potential for rapid price appreciation compared to other indexes. Due to the concentration in technology stocks, QQQ exhibits more price volatility than SPY. Nevertheless, it still provides investors with diversification within the sector. Additionally, the focus on technology can make QQQ more susceptible to sector-specific risks, such as regulatory changes or economic downturns that affect technology companies.

Invesco QQQ ETF Top Holdings (as of August 2024)

Apple (AAPL)

Microsoft (MSFT)

Nvidia Corp. (NVDA)

Broadcom (AVGO)

Amazon (AMZN)

Trading the QQQ ETF, which tracks the Nasdaq-100 Index, can be lucrative given its focus on large-cap technology and growth companies. The QQQ is heavily weighted with Mag-7 equities (Magnificent Seven stocks, also known as the Mag-7, are a group of high-performing and influential companies in the U.S. stock market.)

The average daily trading volume of QQQ is 36 million shares.

Here are some specific trading strategies that investors and traders can use to potentially make money with the QQQ:

Key Technical Indicators:

Momentum traders capitalize on the continuation of existing trends. The QQQ, driven by tech stocks, can exhibit strong momentum in bullish markets.

Bollinger Bands: Given the tech sector's volatility, Bollinger Bands can help identify periods of high volatility and potential breakouts.

MACD (Moving Average Convergence Divergence): A strong indicator for momentum. Look for bullish crossovers for potential long entries.

RSI: Monitor for overbought/oversold conditions. Due to QQQ's volatility, RSI can be particularly effective for identifying overbought and oversold conditions, especially in the short term.

Stochastic Oscillator: Another momentum indicator that can signal overbought or oversold conditions.

Ichimoku Cloud: A comprehensive technical analysis system that can help identify trends, support, and resistance levels.

Strategies:

Breakout Trading: Watch for Bollinger Band squeezes, which typically precede sharp price movements.

Momentum Trading: Utilize MACD crossovers to capture trends in the tech sector.

Sector Rotation: Consider rotating into other sectors during tech sector underperformance or hedging with inverse ETFs. Monitor tech sector performance and rotate into or out of QQQ based on broader market trends.

Options Strategies: Given QQQ's volatility, consider options strategies like covered calls or protective puts.

Covered Call Writing:

Description: This involves selling call options on QQQ while holding the underlying ETF.

Execution: Sell a call option at a strike price above the current QQQ price. Collect the premium, and if QQQ rises above the strike price, your ETF may be called away, but you'll still profit.

Protective Put:

Description: Buy a put option to hedge against a potential decline in QQQ.

Execution: Purchase a put option at a strike price below the current QQQ price to protect against a downside move. If QQQ falls, the put option gains value, offsetting losses in the ETF.

Iron Condor:

Description: A strategy that involves selling an out-of-the-money call and put, while simultaneously buying further out-of-the-money call and put options to limit potential losses.

Execution: If QQQ remains within a certain price range, you collect the premiums from the sold options. This strategy profits from low volatility and a lack of significant price movement.

Beyond the mentioned strategies, here are some additional approaches:

1. Sector Rotation Within Tech

Given the diversity of the tech sector, consider rotating within specific sectors based on performance:

Sector ETFs: Use sector ETFs (e.g., $XLK for technology, $SOXX for semiconductors) to identify outperforming sectors.

Sector Rotation Strategies: Implement strategies like equal-weighting, momentum-based allocation, or thematic investing.

2. ETF-Based Pairs Trading

Pair trading involves simultaneously buying one ETF and selling another with a correlated price movement.

ETF Pairs: To exploit short-term price discrepancies, consider pairing $QQQ with other tech-heavy ETFs or broader market ETFs (e.g., $SPY).

3. Volatility-Based Strategies

Given QQQ's volatility, consider strategies that exploit these fluctuations:

Volatility ETFs: Use volatility ETFs (e.g., $VIX) to hedge against market downturns or profit from increased volatility.

Volatility-Targeted ETFs: Invest in ETFs that aim to maintain a specific level of volatility, regardless of market conditions.

Additional Considerations-

Economic Indicators: Monitor economic indicators like interest rates, consumer spending, and corporate earnings, as they can significantly impact the tech sector.

Regulatory Changes: Monitor regulatory developments, as they can affect tech companies and, in turn, $QQQ's performance. Investors must monitor regulatory news in North America, Europe, and elsewhere.

Global Trends: Pay attention to international trends, such as technological advancements, geopolitical events, and trade tensions, as they can influence the tech sector.

By combining these strategies and factors, investors can make more informed decisions when trading $QQQ and potentially enhance their returns.

If you want to outperform the S&P 500, consider investing in QQQ, otherwise known as the Top 100. It charts the same as SPY but with a wider range because it's literally just the top companies on SPY. If you are a growth oriented, this is the direction to consider.

Chapter 8: $IWM (iShares Russell 2000 ETF)

As a leading ETF tracking the Russell 2000 Index, $IWM provides exposure to U.S. small-cap stocks. The Russell 2000 Index is composed of 2,000 small-cap U.S. stocks, representing the smallest 2,000 companies in the Russell 3000 Index. These companies tend to be more volatile and sensitive to economic conditions than large-cap stocks, making IWM a riskier but potentially higher-reward investment.

IWM provides exposure to small-cap stocks, which are generally companies with market capitalizations between $300 million and $2 billion. These stocks often have higher growth potential than large-cap stocks, as they may be in earlier stages of development. Additionally, stocks within the IWM ETF are typically more volatile than large-cap stocks, meaning investors can expected greater price fluctuations.

IWM ETF Top Holdings (as of August 2024)

Insmed Incorporated (INSM)

FTAI Aviation Ltd. (FTAI)

BLK CSH FND TREASURY SL AGENCY (XTSLA)

Fabrinet (F.N.)

Sprouts Farmers Market, Inc. (SFM)

The average daily trading volume of IWM is 31 million shares.

Key Technical Indicators:

Relative Strength Index (RSI): Small-cap stocks can be more volatile, making RSI an effective tool for timing entries and exits.

Fibonacci Retracement: Use Fibonacci levels to identify key support and resistance areas during retracements.

Volume Oscillator: Analyze the volume oscillator to assess the strength of trends, especially during breakouts or breakdowns.

Bollinger Bands: Can be used to identify overbought and oversold conditions and potential trend reversals.

MACD (Moving Average Convergence Divergence): A momentum indicator that can signal trend changes and potential buy or sell opportunities.

Stochastic Oscillator: Another momentum indicator that measures the speed and change of price movements.

Strategies:

Swing Trading: Use RSI and Fibonacci retracement to identify short-term swings in price.

Risk Management: Given the higher volatility, position sizing, and stop-loss strategies are crucial.

Pairs Trading: Consider pairing IWM with a large-cap ETF like SPY to exploit differences in performance between large and small caps.

Beyond the mentioned strategies, here are some additional approaches:

1. Sector Rotation Within Small-Caps

Given the diversity of the small-cap market, consider rotating within specific sectors based on performance:

Sector ETFs: Use sector ETFs (e.g., $IYY for industrials, $IHF for healthcare) to identify outperforming sectors.

Sector Rotation Strategies: Implement strategies like equal-weighting, momentum-based allocation, or thematic investing.

2. Growth vs. Value Strategies

Small-cap stocks offer both growth and value opportunities:

Growth ETFs: Consider ETFs focusing on growth-oriented small-caps (e.g., $IJS).

Value ETFs: Explore ETFs that target value-oriented small-caps (e.g., $IJS).

3. Momentum Trading

Small-cap stocks can exhibit strong momentum trends:

Momentum Indicators: Use indicators like RSI, MACD, and the Stochastic Oscillator to identify momentum stocks.

Momentum Strategies: Implement strategies like buying stocks that have recently outperformed or selling those that have underperformed.

4. Contrarian Investing

Small-cap stocks can be more susceptible to overreactions, creating potential contrarian opportunities:

Contrarian Indicators: Use indicators like RSI, price-to-book ratio, and price-to-earnings ratio to identify undervalued stocks.

Contrarian Strategies: Invest in stocks that are out of favor but have strong fundamentals.

Additional Considerations

Economic Indicators: Monitor macroeconomic indicators such as GDP growth, interest rates, and consumer confidence, as they can significantly impact small-cap stocks.

Regulatory Changes: Monitor regulatory developments, as they can affect small-cap companies and, in turn, $IWM's performance.

Market Sentiment: Pay attention to market sentiment, as small-cap stocks can be more sensitive to changes in investor sentiment.

By combining these strategies and factors, investors can make more informed decisions when trading $IWM and potentially enhance their returns.

Chapter 9: $EWZ (iShares MSCI Brazil ETF)

As a leading ETF tracking Brazilian equities, $EWZ offers exposure to one of the largest emerging markets. Brazil's economy relies heavily on commodities, making EWZ sensitive to global commodity prices and economic conditions. Additionally, political events and domestic factors can significantly impact its performance.

Brazil has a history of political instability, which can impact its economy and financial markets. Changes in government policies, elections, and social unrest can create uncertainty for investors. Additionally, emerging markets like Brazil are often more susceptible to economic fluctuations than developed economies. Factors such as inflation, interest rates, and currency exchange rates can significantly impact the performance of the Brazilian stock market. The value of the Brazilian Real fluctuates in global currency trading relative to the U.S. dollar. If the Real weakens, the value of your EWZ investment may decline even if the underlying Brazilian stocks are performing well.

With investing in the EWZ, ETF investors experience political risk, currency risk, commodity risk and country economic risk in addition to the risks associated with the Brazilian stocks in the fund.

EWZ ETF Top Holdings (as of August 2024)

CIA Vale Do Rio Doce SH SA (VALE3.SA)

Petroleo Brasileiro Pref SA (PETR4.SA)

Itaú Unibanco Holding Pref SA (ITUB4.SA)

Petroleo Brasileiro Pref SA Petrobras (PETR3.SA)

WEG SA (WEGE3.SA)

The average daily trading volume of EWZ is 22 million shares.

Key Technical Indicators:

Commodity Channel Index (CCI): Given Brazil's reliance on commodities, CCI can be useful for identifying cyclical trends. Brazil is a major exporter, and commodity prices (especially oil and iron ore) significantly impact EWZ.

Currency Strength: Monitor the USD/BRL (Brazilian Real) exchange rate as currency fluctuations can affect ETF performance.

Moving Averages: Crossovers of short and long-term moving averages can help capture trends in emerging markets.

RSI: Monitor overbought/oversold levels, especially during political or economic instability.

While CCI, moving averages, and RSI are valuable tools, here are some additional indicators to consider:

Bollinger Bands: Can be used to identify overbought and oversold conditions and potential trend reversals.

MACD (Moving Average Convergence Divergence): A momentum indicator that can signal trend changes and potential buy or sell opportunities.

Stochastic Oscillator: Another momentum indicator that measures the speed and change of price movements.

Strategies:

Macro Trend Following: Use CCI and moving averages to capture trends driven by commodity prices.

Event-Driven Trading: Take advantage of price movements around political or economic events in Brazil.

Hedging: If investing in EWZ, consider using currency hedges, as currency fluctuations can regularly significantly impact returns in emerging markets and commodities.

Considering market events and your investing time horizon, consider using options or currency ETFs to hedge currency risks relative to the USD/BRL.

Beyond the mentioned strategies, here are some additional approaches:

1. Emerging Markets Rotation

Given the diversity of emerging markets, consider rotating between EWZ and other emerging market ETFs:

Emerging Market ETFs: Explore ETFs that track broader emerging market indices or focus on specific emerging regions.

Emerging Market Rotation: Implement strategies like equal-weighting, momentum-based allocation, or thematic investing.

2. Commodity-Driven Strategies

Brazil's reliance on commodities can offer opportunities for commodity-driven strategies:

Commodity ETFs: Use commodity ETFs (e.g., $USO for oil, $GLD for gold) to capture commodity price trends.

Commodity-Linked Strategies: Consider strategies like pair trading between EWZ and commodity ETFs or using options to hedge against commodity price fluctuations.

3. Country-Specific Analysis

Given the unique dynamics of the Brazilian economy, consider in-depth analysis of country-specific factors:

Economic Indicators: Monitor macroeconomic indicators such as GDP growth, inflation, interest rates, and unemployment.

Political Developments: Stay updated on political events, elections, and policy changes that could impact the Brazilian market.

Corporate Earnings: Analyze corporate earnings reports to identify potential investment opportunities within the Brazilian market.

Additional Considerations-

Currency Fluctuations: The Brazilian Real can be volatile, impacting EWZ's performance. Consider using currency hedging strategies to mitigate currency risk.

Geopolitical Events: Stay updated on global geopolitical events, as they can affect emerging markets, including Brazil.

Market Sentiment: Monitor market sentiment toward emerging markets, as it can influence EWZ's price. Unexpected price volatility can surprise new investors in emerging international markets.

By combining these strategies and factors, investors can make more informed decisions when trading EWZ and potentially enhance their returns.

Chapter 10: $SLV (iShares Silver Trust)

As a leading ETF tracking the price of silver, $SLV offers exposure to this precious metal without needing physical storage. Silver is often viewed as a safe-haven asset. Its price is influenced by factors such as global economic conditions, interest rates, inflation expectations, and industrial demand.

Silver, like gold, has historically been used as a hedge against inflation. When the purchasing power of currency like the U.S. dollar declines, the value of tangible assets like silver often increases. Adding SLV to your personal investment portfolio can help diversify your holdings. Silver has a low correlation with stocks and bonds, which means it can provide a potential hedge against market fluctuations. Silver is used in various industries, including electronics, solar panels, and photography. Growing demand for these applications can drive up the price of silver. Some investors buy SLV based on short-term speculation about future price increases.

SLV ETF Top Holdings (as of August 2024)

Silver 100% (14,491 tons of silver)

The average daily trading volume of SLV is 18 million shares. The IMF (International Monetary Fund), various regulators, and market analysts have recognized that trading in commodity-based ETFs can have a significant affect on the prices of the underlying commodities such as gold, silver and platinum.

Key Technical Indicators:

Moving Averages: The 20-day and 50-day moving averages are particularly useful in a commodity like silver, which can experience sharp price movements.

Relative Strength Index (RSI): Use RSI to identify overbought or oversold conditions, mainly when silver encounters periods of high volatility.

MACD: Utilize MACD for momentum trading, especially during periods of strong trends in the commodity market.

Bollinger Bands: Can be used to identify overbought and oversold conditions and potential trend reversals.

Commodity Channel Index (CCI): A technical indicator designed explicitly for commodities, CCI can help identify cyclical trends in silver prices.

Stochastic Oscillator: Another momentum indicator that measures the speed and change of price movements.

Fibonacci Retracement: Effective in identifying critical support and resistance levels in commodity markets.

Strategies:

Trend Following: Use moving averages to capture trends in silver prices, focusing on global economic indicators that influence precious metals.

Mean Reversion: Silver prices can be mean-reverting; use RSI to identify potential reversal points.

Safe-Haven Play: During periods of economic uncertainty, consider increasing exposure to SLV as a hedge against market volatility.

Beyond the mentioned strategies, here are some additional approaches:

1. Precious Metals Rotation

Given the correlation between silver and other precious metals, consider rotating between SLV and ETFs tracking gold or platinum.

Precious Metal ETFs: Explore ETFs like $GLD for gold and $PLT for platinum.

Rotation Strategies: Implement strategies like equal-weighting, momentum-based allocation, or thematic investing.

2. Industrial Demand Analysis

Silver's industrial demand is a significant driver of its price. Sectors that consume silver include: electronics, solar energy, and photography. Demand and trend analysis can help to gauge potential impacts on silver prices.

3. Inflation Hedging

Supported by historical data, many economists and market analysts view silver as a hedge against inflation.

Inflation Expectations: Monitor inflation reports and economic indicators that could influence inflation. Government inflation data, such as the CPI (Consumer Price Index) report, is issued monthly. Surprises in these reports can produce dramatic short-term price swings and impact your investment portfolio.

Inflation Hedging Strategies: Consider using SLV as a component of a diversified portfolio to hedge against inflation risk.

4. Currency Fluctuations

Currency Correlations: Currency exchange fluctuations can impact silver prices. Analyze correlations between silver and major currencies, such as the U.S. dollar, the euro, and the yen. While the inverse correlation between silver and the U.S. dollar is generally observed, various factors, including specific economic conditions, geopolitical events, and changes in investor sentiment, can influence this relationship. The reasoning behind this is that silver, like other commodities, is priced in U.S. dollars on the global market. The relationship between silver and the euro and the yen is generally less direct compared to the U.S. dollar. Central bank policies and interest rates can affect these correlations.

Currency Hedging: Consider using currency hedging strategies to mitigate currency risk if necessary.

Additional Considerations-

Supply and Demand Dynamics: Monitor global supply and demand trends for silver, including mine production, recycling, and industrial consumption.

Geopolitical Events: Stay updated on geopolitical events affecting silver markets, such as political instability in major silver-producing countries.

The top silver-producing countries in the world are:

Mexico: Mexico has consistently held the top spot in silver production for many years and has a long history of silver mining. In 2023, Mexico's silver mine production reached more than six thousand metric tons. Mexico is blessed with abundant silver deposits, particularly in the Sierra Madre Occidental range and other mineral-rich regions. The country has some of the world's largest silver mines, including the Penasquito and Fresnillo mines, which consistently rank among the top silver-producing mines globally.

China: China is the second-largest silver producer, with production increasing significantly in recent years.

Peru: Peru is another major silver producer known for its rich mineral resources.

Chile: Chile has seen a significant increase in silver production in recent years.

Poland: Poland is a relatively new entrant into the top silver-producing countries.

(Please note that the ranking of countries can change over time due to factors such as economic conditions, technological advancements, and geopolitical events.)

Investor Sentiment: Monitor investor sentiment towards precious metals, which can influence near-term silver prices. The Commitment of Traders (COT) Report is released weekly by the U.S. Commodity Futures Trading Commission (CFTC). The COT report shows the positions held by different types of traders in futures markets, including precious metals. The report divides traders into categories like commercial (hedgers), non-commercial (speculators), and non-reportable (small traders). For example, a high level of long positions by speculators often indicates bullish sentiment, while a high level of short positions can suggest bearish sentiment.

To effectively monitor investor sentiment towards precious metals, it's important to track a combination of these data points and variables. By using a holistic approach that includes futures market data, ETF flows, technical indicators, economic conditions, and sentiment analysis, investors can gain a more comprehensive understanding of how sentiment might influence precious metal prices.

By combining these strategies and factors, investors can make more informed decisions when trading SLV and potentially enhance their returns.

Covered Call Strategy: If you own 100 shares of SLV you could consider the following covered call strategy for income generation (based on market prices, August 2024). With the price of SLV at $27.22 you could consider selling one call at $27.50 for a $1.00 premium, with a one month expiration, which would bring in $100 to your brokerage account (less commissions and fees). The one month return on this transaction would be approximately 3.7%, with an annualized return of 44%, without adjusting for any gain/loss of the underlying stock (assuming the stock is not called away). If the SLV ETF stock is called at $27.50, then your return would be greater. With this example, the investor needs to evaluate the ETFs capital appreciation potential relative to the goal of growth and income prior to engaging in the transaction. If the SLV ETF stock price falls by a couple of dollars, or even remains steady, this strategy then can be viewed as a hedge and the covered call can be sold once again for further income one month later if the investor desires. Of course, if the investor has a trading signal or an opinion that price appreciation of SLV will take place, this covered call option strategy should be avoided.

Investors interested in silver, and specifically the SLV ETF, should research this market well and exercise prudence when investing.

Chapter 11: Selecting the Right ETFs

Investing and selecting ETFs is about customizing a strategy based upon personal goals and risk tolerance.

Understanding Investment Goals: Identify clear investment goals, such as wealth accumulation, income generation, or retirement planning.

Assessing Risk Tolerance: An investor's risk tolerance includes factors like age, financial situation, and comfort level with market fluctuations.

Matching ETFs to Goals and Risk Tolerance: Select ETFs that align with specific investment goals and risk tolerance levels.

Example Scenarios: Illustrate how to choose ETFs for various investment scenarios, such as a young investor seeking growth, a retiree seeking income, or a risk-averse investor.

Chapter 12: Diversification Strategies

Diversification is crucial for managing risk and improving portfolio performance. Nobel Prize economist Harry Markowitz called diversification the one free lunch in investing.

In 2023, the U.S. stock market rose 24%, yet 36% of individual stocks actually lost money (source: Morningstar). If you were an individual investor constructing your own portfolio and were unfortunate to have selected some of those poor performing stocks, the opportunity cost would have been substantial.

Diversifying Across Asset Classes: ETFs can diversify holdings across different asset classes, such as stocks, bonds, commodities, and real estate.

Diversifying Within Asset Classes: Investors should research and explore strategies for diversifying within specific asset classes, such as investing in different sectors, regions, or market cap sizes.

ETF-Based Diversification Portfolios: Diversified ETF portfolios can be tailored to different investment goals and risk tolerances.

Investors should also be aware that too much diversification can limit returns and market opportunities.

General Tips for Trading and Investing in ETFs

Diversification: Even within ETFs, ensure you diversify across different asset classes, sectors, and geographies.

Risk Management: Always use stop-loss orders to manage risk, particularly in volatile ETFs (like $IWM and $EWZ).

Stay Informed: Follow macroeconomic news, as ETFs (like $EWZ and $SLV) are particularly sensitive to global events.

Backtesting: Short-term traders should consider developing and employing backtesting strategies using historical data to see how they would have performed under different market conditions.

Chapter 13: ETFs vs. Index Funds

Exchange-traded funds, or ETFs, and index funds are well-liked financial products that

broad exposure to a range of markets. But there are a few significant distinctions and commonalities as well:

Similarities

Diversification: ETFs and index funds track a specific index, providing broad market exposure.

Low Costs: Both generally have lower expense ratios than actively managed funds.

Passive Management: Most ETFs and index funds are passively managed, meaning they aim to replicate an index's performance rather than outperform it. The largest actively managed ETFs are the JPMorgan Equity Premium Income ETF (JEPI) and the JPMorgan Ultra-Short Income ETF (JPST).

Differences

Trading Flexibility:

ETFs: Trade like stocks on an exchange, allowing investors to buy and sell throughout the trading day at market prices.

Index Funds: These can only be bought or sold at the end of the trading day at the net asset value (NAV) price.

Minimum Investment:

ETFs: Typically have no minimum investment requirement, making them accessible to a broader range of investors. (to be exact, the minimum investment for ETFs is typically one share, although, with some brokerages such as Webull and Robinhood, you can buy fractional shares)

Index Funds: Often have minimum investment requirements, varying by fund.

Tax Efficiency:

ETFs: These funds are generally more tax-efficient due to their unique structure, allowing in-kind redemptions.

Index Funds: They may be less tax-efficient because they might need to sell securities to meet redemptions.

Costs:

ETFs: These funds may incur trading commissions and bid-ask spreads, although many brokers now offer commission-free ETFs.

Index Funds: Typically do not have trading costs but may have higher expense ratios than ETFs.

Dividend Reinvestment:

ETFs: ETFs pay dividends, but how and when they distribute them varies. If an ETF holds dividend-paying stocks, the dividends are typically passed on to investors. Most ETFs distribute dividends quarterly, although some might do so more frequently. Different approaches are taken to handling dividends within ETFs. Some ETFs accumulate dividends in cash until the payout date, while others reinvest them into the fund and distribute them later. Some brokers, including Fidelity, offer options to reinvest dividends commission-free, allowing investors to automatically purchase additional shares with their dividends.

Which Should I Pick?

ETFs are better for investors seeking tax efficiency, reduced expenses, and flexible trading. Index funds are a good option for individuals who want automatic investing and simplicity. Reinvest your dividends to compound returns and make long-term investments free from day-to-day trading.

Which would you rather have, or are you thinking about both?

Chapter 14: ETF Investing for Beginners

Opening a Brokerage Account: Opening a brokerage account is quick and straightforward. Choose a suitable platform that meets your needs.

Understanding ETF Basics: The fundamental concepts of ETFs, including how they work, the different types of ETFs, and the associated costs, are explained throughout this book.

Researching and Selecting ETFs: Tips and strategies for researching ETFs, evaluating their performance, and understanding the underlying holdings are provided throughout this book.

Creating an ETF Portfolio: Building a well-diversified ETF portfolio based on individual investment goals and risk tolerance is important and possible with a personalized and focused investment strategy based upon solid research fundamentals.

Chapter 15: Advanced ETF Strategies

Options Trading with ETFs: Investors should explore using options strategies, such as covered calls, puts, and straddles, to generate income, hedge risk, or speculate on ETF prices. When used correctly and conservatively, option strategies can improve a portfolio's total return.

Arbitrage Opportunities: Strategies can be used to profit from price discrepancies between ETFs and their underlying assets.

ETF-Based Derivatives: Explain the concept of ETF-based derivatives, such as futures and swaps, and their potential uses for hedging or speculating.

Cautionary Notes: The risks associated with advanced ETF strategies can be sustantial. Research and a thorough understanding of individual risk tolerances need to be recognized.

Chapter 16: Recent Trends in ETF Investing

Thematic ETFs and ESG Investing

The ETF landscape has seen a significant shift towards thematic and ESG-focused funds. Investors increasingly seek exposure to specific trends or sectors, such as clean energy, technology, and healthcare. Thematic ETFs offer a targeted way to invest in these areas, aligning with financial goals and personal values. ARK Invest, led by Cathie Wood, is known for its high-conviction bets on disruptive innovation. Despite some volatility, ARK's thematic ETFs have garnered significant attention and inflows. First Trust is another fund recognized for its thematic and sector ETFs, focusing on technology, innovation, and niche markets.

ESG ETFs, which incorporate environmental, social, and governance factors into their investment decisions, have gained traction due to growing investor interest in sustainable investing. These funds aim to generate competitive returns while positively impacting society and the environment.

The iShares ESG Aware MSCI USA ETF (ESGU) is one of the largest and most popular ESG ETFs. It aims to provide exposure to U.S. companies that have high ESG ratings while maintaining a similar risk and return profile to the broader U.S. equity market. Its expense ratio is 0.15%. Another ESG fund is the Vanguard ESG U.S. Stock ETF (ESGV). This ETF provides broad exposure to U.S. companies that meet specific ESG criteria, avoiding companies involved in certain industries like tobacco, fossil fuels, and weapons. It includes a diverse range of large, mid, and small-cap companies in the United States. The expense ratio is 0.09%.

Smart Beta Strategies

Smart beta strategies have also become more prevalent in the ETF space. These strategies deviate from traditional market-cap-weighted indexes, often using factors like quality, value, or momentum to select securities. By focusing on these factors, smart beta ETFs aim to capture potential alpha and reduce tracking errors compared to traditional index funds. J.P. Morgan has been expanding its ETF offerings rapidly, focusing on active and strategic beta products with solid inflows in recent years.

Record ETF Inflows info Funds

The popularity of ETFs is evident in the continued strong inflows over the past several years. The July 2024 inflow of $122 billion highlights the growing investor preference for ETFs as a convenient and efficient investment vehicle. This trend will persist as investors seek diversification, low costs, and exposure to various asset classes and strategies.

Key Takeaways

Thematic ETFs are gaining popularity as investors seek targeted exposure to specific trends or sectors.

ESG-focused ETFs are attracting investor interest due to the growing demand for sustainable investing.

Smart beta strategies offer alternative weighting methodologies to traditional market-cap-weighted indexes.

ETF inflows continue to be strong, indicating growing investor preference for ETFs.

The ongoing evolution of the ETF market suggests that investors can expect to see even more innovative and targeted products in the future as issuers strive to meet their clients evolving needs and preferences.

The popularity of exchange-traded funds, with thematic and ESG-focused investing, is at an all-time high.

Chapter 17: Cryptocurrency ETFs

Yes, there are ETFs with cryptocurrencies, though they are relatively new and have certain nuances compared to traditional ETFs. Here are the key points to understand:

1. Cryptocurrency ETFs:

Bitcoin and Ethereum ETFs: Some of the most notable cryptocurrency ETFs are those that track the performance of Bitcoin and Ethereum, the two largest cryptocurrencies by market capitalization. These ETFs either hold the actual cryptocurrency (physical ETFs) or track futures contracts or other financial instruments that derive their value from the cryptocurrency (futures-based ETFs).

Physical ETFs: These ETFs hold actual units of the cryptocurrency in a custodial account. This means that when you buy a share of the ETF, you're essentially buying a portion of the cryptocurrency held by the fund. As of now, physical cryptocurrency ETFs are more common in jurisdictions like Canada and Europe.

Futures-Based ETFs: In the U.S., the first approved cryptocurrency ETFs were futures-based, meaning they track Bitcoin or Ethereum futures rather than the actual cryptocurrencies. These were introduced to mitigate the regulatory concerns associated with holding physical cryptocurrencies.

Examples:

ProShares Bitcoin Strategy ETF (BITO): This was the first Bitcoin futures ETF approved in the U.S. in October 2021. It tracks Bitcoin futures contracts rather than the spot price of Bitcoin.

Purpose Bitcoin ETF (BTCC): This is a Canadian ETF that holds actual Bitcoin, making it the first physically-backed Bitcoin ETF in the world.

VanEck Ethereum Strategy ETF (EFUT): This is an Ethereum futures-based ETF that provides exposure to Ethereum futures contracts.

2. Challenges and Considerations:

Regulation: The introduction of cryptocurrency ETFs has been slow in some regions, particularly the U.S., due to regulatory concerns about the volatility, security, and manipulation of cryptocurrency markets.

Volatility: Cryptocurrency ETFs can be highly volatile due to the nature of the underlying assets. Investors need to be prepared for significant price swings.

Fees: Cryptocurrency ETFs tend to have higher management fees compared to traditional ETFs, partly due to the complexity of managing the assets and the higher risk involved.

3. Global Adoption:

Canada and Europe: These regions have been more open to approving physically-backed cryptocurrency ETFs. Several

Bitcoin and Ethereum ETFs are available in Canada and certain European markets.

United States: The U.S. has taken a more cautious approach, with the Securities and Exchange Commission (SEC) approving only futures-based ETFs so far. However, there is ongoing discussion and interest in potentially approving physically-backed cryptocurrency ETFs in the future.

4. Diversified Cryptocurrency ETFs:

Blockchain and Cryptocurrency-Themed ETFs: Some ETFs do not invest directly in cryptocurrencies but instead focus on companies involved in the blockchain technology or cryptocurrency ecosystem. These ETFs offer exposure to the broader sector without directly holding cryptocurrencies.

Examples:

Amplify Transformational Data Sharing ETF (BLOK): Invests in companies involved in blockchain technology.

Global X Blockchain ETF (BKCH): Focuses on companies that benefit from blockchain technologies.

Cryptocurrency ETFs are a growing segment of the ETF market, offering investors exposure to the volatile and rapidly evolving world of digital assets. In 2024 the market has witnessed significant crypto adoption by institutional investors and brokerages such as BlackRock, Fidelity and Robinhood. While there are still regulatory hurdles and risks to consider, these ETFs provide a more accessible and regulated way for investors to gain exposure to cryptocurrencies without directly owning them.

Many financial advisors will inform investors that purchasing cryptocurrency (in any form) is speculation, not investing. When building a portfolio, it would be generally wise to limit the percentage devoted to crypto in a given portfolio for risk managment reasons.

Chapter 18: Avoiding Mistakes

Let's dive deeper into each of the top ten ETF investing mistakes, with examples, strategies for correction, and how avoiding these pitfalls can lead to better long-term profits.

1. Overlooking the Expense Ratio

Example: An investor chooses an actively managed ETF with a 1% expense ratio over a passive index ETF with a 0.05% expense ratio because the active ETF had a strong performance last year.

Correction: Always compare expense ratios before investing. Opt for lower-cost ETFs, especially in markets where high returns are not guaranteed.

Long-Term Benefit: Lower costs mean more of your money is working for you, which can significantly compound over time, especially in low-growth periods.

2. Ignoring the ETF's Underlying Assets

Example: An investor buys a high-yield bond ETF without realizing it is heavily weighted in junk bonds, (speculative-grade bonds) which carry higher risk.

Correction: Research the ETF's holdings and ensure they align with your risk tolerance and investment goals. Tools like Morningstar or the ETF's own prospectus can provide detailed breakdowns and bond quality ratings.

Long-Term Benefit: Aligning your investments with your risk tolerance reduces the likelihood of panic-selling during downturns, improving long-term returns.

3. Chasing Performance

Example: After seeing a technology ETF surge 50% in the last year, an investor buys in, only to see it drop by 20% during a market correction.

Correction: Focus on long-term performance and fundamentals, rather than short-term gains. Consider dollar-cost averaging to avoid buying high.

Long-Term Benefit: By avoiding performance-chasing, you reduce the chances of buying at market peaks and increase the likelihood of capturing gains during market recoveries.

4. Neglecting Liquidity

Example: An investor buys an ETF with a low average daily volume, leading to a large bid-ask spread. When they sell, they get a price significantly lower than expected.

Correction: Check the ETF's average trading volume and bid-ask spread. Stick to ETFs with high liquidity, especially if you plan to trade frequently.

Long-Term Benefit: High liquidity allows for smoother entry and exit from positions, reducing transaction costs and preserving more of your investment capital.

5. Failing to Diversify

Example: An investor puts all their money into a biotech ETF, believing the sector will outperform due to new drug approvals. When the sector faces regulatory setbacks, their portfolio tanks.

Correction: Diversify across asset classes, sectors, and geographies. Use a mix of ETFs to spread risk, such as combining equity, bond, and commodity ETFs.

Long-Term Benefit: Diversification reduces the impact of poor performance in any single sector, leading to more stable returns over time.

6. Ignoring Tax Implications

Example: An investor frequently trades ETFs in a taxable account, resulting in short-term capital gains, which are taxed at a higher rate.

Correction: Be mindful of tax-efficient strategies, like holding ETFs long-term to benefit from lower long-term capital gains taxes. Consider tax-loss harvesting to offset gains.

Long-Term Benefit: Efficient tax management allows you to keep more of your returns, boosting your overall portfolio growth.

7. Not Understanding the ETF's Structure

Example: An investor buys a leveraged ETF to hold long-term, not realizing that it is designed for short-term trading and rebalances daily, leading to significant tracking errors over time.

Correction: Understand the structure and intended use of the ETF. Leveraged and inverse ETFs are typically for short-term trades, not long-term holds.

Long-Term Benefit: Using ETFs as intended helps avoid unexpected losses and aligns your strategy with the product's strengths.

8. Timing the Market

Example: An investor sells an equity ETF during a market downtrend or dip, fearing further losses, and then misses out on the subsequent recovery.

Correction: Focus on long-term goals rather than short-term market movements. Dollar-cost averaging and maintaining a disciplined investment approach can help mitigate the urge to time the market.

Long-Term Benefit: Staying invested during market downturns allows you to benefit from rebounds, leading to better long-term returns.

9. Ignoring the ETF's Tracking Error

Example: An investor expects an ETF to mirror the S&P 500, but due to high tracking error, the ETF underperforms the index by 1-2% annually.

Correction: Review the ETF's tracking error before investing. Choose ETFs with low tracking error to ensure they closely follow the intended index.

Long-Term Benefit: Low tracking error ensures your ETF performs as expected, helping you meet your investment objectives more reliably.

10. Overlooking the Importance of Rebalancing

Example: An investor's portfolio becomes overweight in technology stocks as they outperform, but they don't rebalance. When the tech sector declines, the portfolio suffers significant losses.

Correction: Regularly review and rebalance your portfolio to maintain your desired asset allocation. Automated rebalancing services can also help.

Long-Term Benefit: Rebalancing ensures your portfolio stays aligned with your risk tolerance and goals, reducing the risk of large losses in any one sector.

Conclusion

Learning from these common mistakes, through self-education and strong research practices, and implementing the corrections can help investors protect their portfolios from avoidable losses, reduce costs, and maximize returns. Consistently applying these strategies leads to a more disciplined investment approach, increasing the likelihood of achieving long-term financial success.

Chapter 19: Build Wealth Investors!

The way that institutions and people invest has changed dramatically because of exchange-traded funds (ETFs). They are an effective and adaptable instrument in the investor's toolbox, providing a number of advantages like cost effectiveness, tax advantages, and liquidity. But not every ETF is made equal, and it's important to to fully investigate and comprehend the unique features of any ETF before making an investment. Investors might evaluate cost, liquidity, tax consequences, and management style make better judgments and match their ETF investments to their financial objectives.

To properly manage risk and capitalize on market opportunities, investors must comprehend the subtle differences between various exchange-traded funds (ETFs). Examples of these include broad index tracking ETFs like SPY and QQQ, and more specialized markets like EWZ and SLV. ETFs have many appealing features for both long-term investors as well as for short-term traders.

ETFs are superior to mutual funds in a number of ways, including lower costs, trading flexibility, potential tax benefits, and other aspects. There are many positive advantages for investors in ETFs.

Continuous learning about investments is always an important financial activity. It should never be just an occasional endeavor. We encourage readers to stay informed about the ETF market and explore new investment opportunities as they arise. Keep up with market trends, news, and economic indicators that could impact your ETF holdings. Stay informed and monitor your investments. An attitude of benign neglect regarding your investment holdings can adversely affect your portfolio's performance.

Call to Action: We encourage readers to proceed with their ETF investing by creating a brokerage account (if not already in place), learning more about ETFs, or speaking with a financial advisor. Also recommended is for investors to regularly review and rebalance your portfolio to ensure it aligns with your investment goals and risk tolerance. Rebalancing might involve buying or selling ETFs to maintain your desired asset allocation mix.

A simple and brilliant investment strategy is to invest a fixed dollar amount of every paycheck into one or more ETFs within your portfolio. This disciplined approach will take advantage of dollar-cost averaging and much more. In five or ten year you will thank yourself enormously.

With 78% of all Americans having saved $50,000 or less for retirement, investing wisely becomes more critical than ever before.

We wish every ETF investor the best of luck and prosperity!

Appendix A: Glossary of ETF Terms

Active Management

Active management is an investment strategy where a professional fund manager or team seeks to outperform a specific benchmark index by making active decisions about buying and selling securities. Active managers use research, forecasts, and their own judgment to decide which securities to buy, hold, or sell. Funds which employ an active management investment strategy incur higher expense ratios due to higher portfolio turnover.

Alpha

Alpha is a measure of a portfolio's excess return compared to its expected return based on its level of risk. A positive alpha indicates the portfolio outperformed its benchmark, while a negative alpha suggests underperformance.

Asset Allocation

Asset allocation is the strategy of dividing your investment portfolio among different asset classes (like stocks, bonds, and cash) to manage risk and return. The goal of asset allocation is to optimize the risk/reward profile of a portfolio according to an investor's time horizon, risk tolerance, and financial goals. It helps balance your portfolio's exposure to different types of investments.

Diversification

Diversification is spreading your investments across various assets to reduce risk. It helps mitigate the impact of a downturn in any particular asset class.

Expense Ratio

The expense ratio is the annual fee that all funds or ETFs charge their shareholders. It is a percentage of the fund's average assets under management (AUM). For example, an ETF with an expense ratio of 0.20% would cost $2 annually for every $1,000 invested. All investors should research and pay close attention to expense ratios for ETFs.

Importance: A lower expense ratio is preferable as a smaller portion of your investment goes toward management fees, allowing more of your investment to grow over time.

Itemized below are the five ETFs identified in this book. ETFs linked to major indexes typically have very low expense ratios.

$SPY 0.095%

$QQQ 0.200%

$IWM 0.190%

$EWZ 0.590%

$SLV 0.500%

(Be aware that expense ratios can and do change over time. The above noted expense ratio data is from August 2024).

An ETF's expense ratio can be easily and quickly identified online when searched for at major financial websites.

ETFs are often lauded for their lower expense ratios when compared with other investment vehicles like mutual funds. Over the years, the decline in expense ratios is a testament to the competitive pressure that has driven costs down across the board. However, the notion that all ETFs are inexpensive is a common misconception.

Exchange-Traded Fund (ETF)

An **ETF** is a type of investment fund that pools money from investors to buy a basket of securities. ETFs are traded on stock exchanges like individual stocks, offering flexibility and liquidity. They can track various indexes, sectors, or commodities.

In-Kind Redemption

In-kind redemption is the process by which institutional investors can exchange ETF shares for the underlying securities in the fund rather than cash. This mechanism helps maintain tax efficiency and reduces the need for the fund to sell securities, which could trigger capital gains. This process is key to ETFs' tax efficiency, making them a more attractive option for investors seeking to minimize capital gains distributions.

Investment Liquidity

Investment liquidity refers to how easily you can buy or sell an investment without significantly affecting its price. ETFs generally offer high liquidity due to their trading on stock exchanges.

Market Capitalization

Market capitalization, or "market cap," is the total market value of a company's outstanding shares of stock. In the context of ETFs, market cap is used to categorize the underlying stocks in the fund, such as large-cap, mid-cap, or small-cap ETFs.

Importance: Knowing the market cap of an ETF's holdings can help investors align their investment strategies with their risk tolerance. Large-cap stocks tend to be more stable, while small-cap stocks may offer higher growth potential but with more risk.

Net Asset Value (NAV)

The NAV is the per-share value of an ETF's assets minus its liabilities. It is calculated at the end of each trading day. Like a company's book value, NAV assesses whether an ETF trades at a premium or discount on its underlying assets. Understanding NAV helps investors determine the true value of their ETF holdings and make informed decisions about buying or selling shares.

Passive Investment

Passive investment involves tracking a market index. An investment strategy that seeks to replicate the performance of a specific index or benchmark, such as the S&P 500, rather than trying to outperform it. Passive investing typically involves buying an index fund or ETF that tracks the performance of the chosen benchmark. Very low fund expense ratios are associated with passive investing due to infrequent portfolio turnover.

Risk

Risk is the potential for loss or the uncertainty regarding the future returns of an investment. Risk can arise from various factors, including market volatility, economic changes, and company-specific events. It can be measured in terms of volatility or standard deviation. Beta analysis, as a proxy for risk, is considered an outdated financial tool. The risk-return tradeoff (a direct, positive relationship) is a fundamental concept in financial management.

S&P 500 Index

The **S&P 500 Index** is a widely used benchmark that tracks the stock performance of 500 large companies in the United States. It's often seen as a representation of the overall U.S. stock market. It is a better market index than the Dow Jones Industrial Average (DJIA). One criticism of this index is that it is too heavily weighted with a limited group of popular technology companies (such as Microsoft, Google, Meta, etc.)

Sector Investing

Sector investing involves focusing on a specific industry or economic sector (like technology, healthcare, or energy). Sector investing allows investors to target areas of the market that they believe will outperform others based on economic or market trends.

Tracking Error

Tracking error measures the divergence between an ETF's performance and its benchmark index. It is typically expressed as the standard deviation of the difference between the fund's and index's returns and can significantly impact returns.

Importance: A low tracking error is crucial for investors looking to mirror the performance of indices like the S&P 500®. Additionally, the bid-ask spread—the difference between the price buyers are willing to pay and the price sellers are willing to accept—can add to the cost of trading ETFs. ETFs with wider bid-ask spreads can be more expensive to trade, making it crucial to evaluate these factors alongside expense ratios when assessing the actual cost of an ETF.

Volatility

Volatility refers to the degree of fluctuation in an investment's price over time. A statistical measure of the dispersion of returns for a given security or market index. Volatility represents the degree of variation in an asset's price over time, with higher volatility indicating greater price swings and more risk. It is often used as a measure of market risk.

Appendix B: Investor Profile of ETF Investors

Research on the average profile of an ETF (Exchange-Traded Fund) investor reveals several key characteristics. While there's no one-size-fits-all profile, research suggests that ETF investors tend to share specific characteristics.

Here's an overview of what studies and surveys typically show:

1. Demographics

Age: ETF investors tend to be younger than mutual fund investors. Many studies indicate that the average ETF investor is in their 30s to 40s.

Income: ETF investors generally have higher incomes. They often belong to middle to upper-middle-income brackets, indicating a higher level of financial sophistication.

Education: A significant portion of ETF investors have a college degree, with many holding advanced degrees, suggesting a strong understanding of financial concepts.

2. Investment Experience

Sophistication: ETF investors are typically more financially literate and experienced than average retail investors. They are more likely to engage in self-directed investing.

Technology Usage: They tend to be more tech-savvy, using online platforms and tools for trading and research.

3. Investment Behavior

Diversification: ETF investors appreciate diversification and often use ETFs as part of a broader portfolio strategy. They value the ability to invest in a broad range of bundled assets with a single trade.

Cost Sensitivity: ETF investors are typically cost-conscious, favoring ETFs due to their lower expense ratios than mutual funds.

Risk Tolerance: They generally exhibit a moderate to high-risk tolerance, given that ETFs can be used for more aggressive strategies, including sector-specific and leveraged ETFs.

Frequent trading: Some ETF investors are more driven by short-term market and trading opportunities.

4. Motivations

Flexibility: The ability to trade ETFs like stocks, with intraday pricing, appeals to these investors.

Transparency: Many ETF investors value the transparency of ETFs' holdings and fees compared to other investment vehicles.

5. Portfolio Composition

Core-Satellite Strategy: Many ETF investors use a core-satellite approach, where ETFs form the core of the portfolio, with individual stocks or more specialized ETFs as satellites.

Sector and Thematic Investing: ETF investors often pursue specific sectors or themes, such as technology, clean energy, or international markets, leveraging the variety of ETFs available.

6. Geographic and Psychographic Aspects

Geography: ETF investors are more prevalent in developed markets like the U.S., Europe, and Australia. However, their adoption is growing globally.

Psychographics: They tend to be more proactive and engaged in managing their investments, often consuming financial news and research.

7. Trends

The profile of ETF investors is broadening, with increasing adoption across different age groups and income levels, partly due to the growing popularity of ETFs in retirement accounts and with robo-advisors.

These insights help to understand who is investing in ETFs and why they prefer them over other investment vehicles.

Appendix C: Top 50 ETFs by Assets Under Management (AUM)

The most recent data shows the top 50 ETFs ranked by assets under management (AUM). These ETFs cover a range of asset classes, including equities, bonds, and commodities. The rankings may change as markets fluctuate, so these figures represent a snapshot:

1. SPDR S&P 500 ETF Trust ($SPY)

Category: U.S. Large-Cap

2. iShares Core S&P 500 ETF ($IVV)

Category: U.S. Large-Cap

3. Vanguard Total Stock Market ETF ($VTI)

Category: U.S. Total Market

4. Vanguard S&P 500 ETF ($VOO)

Category: U.S. Large-Cap

5. Invesco QQQ Trust ($QQQ)

Category: U.S. Large-Cap Growth (Tech-Heavy)

6. Vanguard FTSE Developed Markets ETF ($VEA)

Category: International Developed Markets

7. iShares MSCI Emerging Markets ETF ($EEM)

Category: Emerging Markets

8. Vanguard FTSE Emerging Markets ETF ($VWO)

Category: Emerging Markets

9. iShares Core U.S. Aggregate Bond ETF ($AGG)

Category: U.S. Bonds

10. iShares Russell 2000 ETF ($IWM)

Category: U.S. Small-Cap

11. Vanguard Total Bond Market ETF ($BND)

Category: U.S. Bonds

12. SPDR Gold Shares ($GLD)

Category: Commodities (Gold)

13. iShares MSCI EAFE ETF ($EFA)

Category: International Developed Markets

14. Vanguard Real Estate ETF ($VNQ)

Category: Real Estate

15. Vanguard Growth ETF ($VUG)

Category: U.S. Large-Cap Growth

16. Vanguard Value ETF ($VTV)

Category: U.S. Large-Cap Value

17. Vanguard High Dividend Yield ETF ($VYM)

Category: U.S. Large-Cap Dividend

18. iShares Core MSCI EAFE ETF ($IEFA)

Category: International Developed Markets

19. iShares 20+ Year Treasury Bond ETF ($TLT)

Category: U.S. Treasury Bonds

20. iShares Core S&P Small-Cap ETF ($IJR)

Category: U.S. Small-Cap

21. SPDR Portfolio S&P 500 ETF ($SPLG)

Category: U.S. Large-Cap

22. Schwab U.S. Broad Market ETF ($SCHB)

Category: U.S. Total Market

23. iShares Core MSCI Emerging Markets ETF ($IEMG)

Category: Emerging Markets

24. Vanguard Dividend Appreciation ETF ($VIG)

Category: U.S. Dividend

25. iShares MBS ETF ($MBB)

Category: U.S. Mortgage-Backed Securities

26. SPDR Bloomberg Barclays High Yield Bond ETF ($JNK)

Category: U.S. High Yield Bonds

27. iShares U.S. Real Estate ETF ($IYR)

Category: Real Estate

28. Vanguard Information Technology ETF ($VGT)

Category: U.S. Sector (Technology)

29. Vanguard Mid-Cap ETF ($ V.O.)

Category: U.S. Mid-Cap

30. iShares MSCI USA Min Vol Factor ETF ($USMV)

Category: U.S. Large-Cap (Low Volatility)

31. iShares iBoxx $ Investment Grade Corporate Bond ETF ($LQD)

Category: U.S. Corporate Bonds

32. Vanguard Small-Cap ETF ($ V.B.)

Category: U.S. Small-Cap

33. iShares Russell 1000 Growth ETF ($IWF)

Category: U.S. Large-Cap Growth

34. iShares Russell 1000 Value ETF ($IWD)

Category: U.S. Large-Cap Value

35. Vanguard FTSE All-World ex-US ETF ($VEU)

Category: International Ex-U.S.

36. Invesco Preferred ETF ($PGX)

Category: Preferred Shares

37. Schwab International Equity ETF ($SCHF)

Category: International Developed Markets

38. Vanguard Intermediate-Term Bond ETF ($BIV)

Category: U.S. Bonds

39. iShares Core U.S. REIT ETF ($USRT)

Category: Real Estate

40. Vanguard Financials ETF ($VFH)

Category: U.S. Sector (Financials)

41. Vanguard Communication Services ETF ($VOX)

Category: U.S. Sector (Communication Services)

42. Vanguard Consumer Discretionary ETF ($VCR)

Category: U.S. Sector (Consumer Discretionary)

43. iShares Core Dividend Growth ETF ($DGRO)

Category: U.S. Dividend Growth

44. Vanguard Utilities ETF ($VPU)

Category: U.S. Sector (Utilities)

45. iShares Edge MSCI Min Vol USA ETF ($USMV)

Category: U.S. Low Volatility

46. SPDR Portfolio Aggregate Bond ETF ($SPAB)

Category: U.S. Bonds

47. Vanguard Health Care ETF ($VHT)

Category: U.S. Sector (Healthcare)

48. Invesco S&P 500 Equal Weight ETF ($RSP)

Category: U.S. Large-Cap

49. Vanguard Short-Term Bond ETF ($BSV)

Category: U.S. Bonds

50.

Schwab U.S. Dividend Equity ETF ($SCHD)

Category: U.S. Dividend

These ETFs are popular due to their liquidity, low expense ratios, and their wide range of exposure to various markets and sectors. The exact rankings and AUM figures may vary depending on the source and the data date. (circa 2023)

BlackRock's iShares is the largest ETF provider globally, and it is known for its extensive range of products, including equity and bond ETFs.

Appendix D: Top 5 Lowest Cost Major ETFs

The expense ratio calculation for funds is critical for investors to determine, as lower costs can significantly enhance long-term returns. Here are five of the major ETFs with the lowest expense ratios:

1. Vanguard S&P 500 ETF (VOO)

Expense Ratio: 0.03%

Description: VOO tracks the S&P 500 index, providing exposure to 500 of the largest U.S. companies. It's one of the most cost-effective ways to invest in a broad segment of the U.S. equity market.

2. iShares Core S&P 500 ETF (IVV)

Expense Ratio: 0.03%

Description: Similar to VOO, IVV also tracks the S&P 500. It offers the same broad exposure to large-cap U.S. stocks with a very low expense ratio.

3. SPDR S&P 500 ETF Trust (SPY)

Expense Ratio: 0.095%

Description: SPY is one of the most popular and widely traded ETFs, tracking the S&P 500 index. While slightly more expensive than VOO and IVV, it still offers very low costs.

4. Vanguard Total Stock Market ETF (VTI)

Expense Ratio: 0.03%

Description: VTI provides exposure to the entire U.S. stock market, including large, mid, small, and micro-cap stocks. It's a comprehensive, low-cost option for broad U.S. equity exposure.

5. Schwab U.S. Broad Market ETF (SCHB)

Expense Ratio: 0.03%

Description: SCHB offers minimal cost exposure to the broad U.S. stock market, covering over 2,500 stocks across large, mid, and small-cap sectors.

These ETFs are among the lowest-cost options available, making them attractive for investors looking to minimize expenses while gaining exposure to key market segments.

Appendix E: Quotes from financial leaders in the ETF sector

Larry Fink (Chairman and CEO, BlackRock):

"ETFs are the future of asset management. They offer investors access to a broad range of assets cost-effectively and transparently. The innovation and efficiency they bring to the market have revolutionized how people invest."

Tim Buckley (Chairman and CEO, Vanguard):

"ETFs have democratized investing by providing low-cost, diversified access to global markets. For long-term investors, they offer a simple, efficient way to build wealth over time."

Cathie Wood (Founder, CEO, and CIO, ARK Invest):

"We believe ETFs are the perfect vehicle for disruptive innovation. They allow investors to access high-growth potential areas of the market that were previously inaccessible or difficult to invest in."

Cyrus Taraporevala (President and CEO, State Street Global Advisors):

"The SPDR S&P 500 ETF Trust ($SPY) wasn't just the first ETF; it laid the foundation for what has become a $7 trillion industry. ETFs are a critical tool for investors, offering liquidity, transparency, and cost efficiency."

Martin L. Flanagan (President and CEO, Invesco):

"ETFs provide flexibility and precision for investors looking to tailor their portfolios to specific investment needs or themes. As the market evolves, ETFs will continue to play a key role in how investors achieve their goals."

These quotes highlight ETFs' significant impact on the financial industry, emphasizing their role in democratizing investment, offering flexibility, and providing innovative solutions for many investors.

Appendix F: Dividend ETFs

ETFs which provide the benefits of growth and income include Dividend ETFs.

ETFs pay dividends, but how and when they distribute them varies. If an ETF holds dividend-paying stocks, the dividends are typically passed on to investors. Most ETFs distribute dividends quarterly, although some might do so more frequently. Investors should review an ETF's prospectus to understand its dividend distribution policy, as this can affect income streams and reinvestment strategies.

Examples of stocks which combine these features and goals (growth and income) are Home Depot, JPMorgan Chase, Coca-Cola and others that are included within the following ETFs. Each of the following funds report ten-year annual returns of at least 10%. (The data below is circa August 2024)

charles SCHWAB	iShares	Vanguard
US Dividend Equity	*Dividend Growth*	*High Dividend*
SCHD	DGRO	VYM
Dividend Yield 3.7%	Dividend Yield 2.31%	Dividend Yield 2.71%
Expense Ratio 0.06%	Expense Ratio 0.08%	Expense Ratio 0.06%

Appendix G: Resources for Further Research

Reliable Websites:

Morningstar: www.morningstar.com

Offers comprehensive ETF research, including ratings, performance data, and analysis.

Yahoo Finance: finance.yahoo.com

A popular platform for tracking ETF prices, performance, and news. It also offers basic analytical tools.

Investopedia: www.investopedia.com

Provides educational content on ETFs, including definitions, strategy guides, and investment advice.

Fidelity: www.fidelity.com

Fidelity's website offers detailed information on ETFs, including tools for screening and comparing different funds.

Lipper: www.lipperleaders.com

Ranks funds by 5 characteristics.

www.ingramcontent.com/pod-product-compliance
Lightning Source LLC
Chambersburg PA
CBHW051246160726
47994CB00003B/1043

DEDICATION

This book is lovingly dedicated to the Father of Love, who loved before creation began; to the Son, Jesus Christ, the visible expression of that Love; and to the Holy Spirit, who pours that same Love into our hearts.

It is also dedicated to all who hunger to know God not as an idea, but as Love Himself — to those who have been broken, searching, and waiting to understand that every pain, every promise, and every prayer is part of a love story that began in eternity and will never end.

May every word in these pages draw you nearer to His heart, where the mystery of Love becomes life itself.

ABOUT THE AUTHOR

Peter Lengwe is a passionate student of the Word of God, moved deeply by the revelation of God's love and the mystery of His eternal plan. His life and ministry are rooted in one enduring pursuit — to know Christ and to make Him known through the truth of Scripture and the power of the Holy Spirit.

From an early age, Peter's heart was captivated by the beauty of the Bible. Yet, through years of study and prayer, he discovered that at the center of every verse, every story, and every prophecy stands one word that defines them all — Love.

Out of this revelation came The Mystery of Love — a book not born from theory, but from worship, devotion, and a lifelong encounter with the living God. Peter's desire is not merely to inform, but to awaken hearts; to help believers understand that love is not a feeling or concept, but the very essence of God Himself.

Each page of this book carries the heartbeat of Scripture — from creation to the cross, from the Holy Spirit's outpouring to the final union of the Bride and the Lamb. It is Peter's prayer that readers will not only learn about love but will experience it — that they will encounter the Father's heart, the Son's sacrifice, and the Spirit's indwelling presence in a deeper, transforming way.

Peter's writing is marked by a blend of reverence and clarity — combining the depth of biblical revelation with the tenderness of divine invitation. He believes that every Christian, regardless of background, is called to live in the fullness of love: to receive it, reflect it, and return it to the Father who first gave it.

The Mystery of Love continues Peter's calling to reveal biblical truth with conviction and compassion, helping the Church rediscover what it means to walk in love, to endure in love, and to be perfected in love.

His hope is that this book becomes not just a message, but a movement — a call to return to the first love, where every act of faith, every sacrifice, and every word of worship flows from a heart that truly knows the Father.

For Peter, love is not just theology — it is destiny.

And that destiny is found only in Christ.

Table of Contents

PREFACE

Unfolding the Eternal Purpose of God Through the Power of Love

This book was born out of a longing — not merely to understand God, but to know His heart.

The Bible declares, "God is love" (1 John 4:8, NKJV).

These three words, simple as they sound, contain the depth of eternity. They are not a definition, but a revelation — for to know God is to know love, and to know love is to behold the very essence of who He is.

For generations, humanity has sought to define love through emotion, desire, and reason. But divine love — agapē — is not rooted in human affection; it is the self-giving nature of God that transcends all understanding.

It is love that creates, love that redeems, love that disciplines, and love that endures.

From Genesis to Revelation, the Word of God unfolds this mystery:

that every act of creation, every covenant, every commandment, and every drop of blood shed upon the cross flows from one eternal source — the heart of Love Himself.

Love is not God's attribute; it is His identity. It is the breath that spoke the universe into being, the compassion that reached down to fallen man, and the power that raised Jesus Christ from the grave.

Yet the mystery of love is not only in how God loves us, but in how we are called to love Him in return.

This is the divine exchange that completes the circle of eternity — the Creator and the created united again through the power of love.

The purpose of this book is not to discuss love as an idea, but to decode love according to the Word of God — to unveil the dimensions of divine love in its purity, purpose, and power. It is an invitation to walk through Scripture not as a student of theology, but as a seeker of the heart of God.

Every chapter you read will lead you deeper — from the meaning of love in Hebrew and Greek, to the commandment of love among believers, to the union of love in marriage and family, and finally to the eternal love between the Father and His children.

This journey is both revelation and reflection.

It is for those who desire not just to know about God's love, but to be transformed by it.

My prayer is that as you turn each page, you will feel the Father drawing you closer — past doctrine and tradition, into the living presence of the One who is Love Himself.

May this book open your eyes to see that the mystery is not hidden — it has always been revealed in Christ Jesus.

And as you read, may your heart echo the eternal truth:

"We love Him because He first loved us."
— 1 John 4:19, NKJV

INTRODUCTION

From the dawn of creation to the final pages of Revelation, one truth echoes through eternity: God is Love.

These three words seem simple, yet they contain within them the fullness of divine mystery. Love is not merely an emotion, nor is it a passing virtue—it is the very essence of God's being, the foundation of His purpose, and the reason all things exist.

Before there was light, before angels sang, before man ever breathed—Love was.

Love existed eternally in the fellowship of the Father, the Son, and the Holy Spirit. From this divine communion flowed creation itself. Every star that shines, every heartbeat that pulses, every breath drawn in wonder—all originate from that endless river of divine affection.

Yet, this love was not content to remain hidden.

It desired to be known, to be shared, to be revealed. The mystery of love is that the infinite God desired relationship with the finite, that He would create beings capable of both receiving and returning His love.

But love, by its very nature, allows choice. And where choice exists, rejection is possible.

When man turned away from God, it seemed that love had been wounded. Yet even in that moment, love began its greatest revelation. Through every covenant, through every prophet, through every act of mercy, God was writing a story of love's pursuit—a story that would culminate in the giving of Himself.

On the cross, the mystery of love was unveiled.

There, infinite holiness met infinite mercy. There, justice and compassion embraced. And there, Love Himself hung between heaven and earth, proving once and for all that love is not defined by what it gains, but by what it gives.

This book is a journey into that mystery.

It seeks to decode love—not through the shallow definitions of this world, but through the living Word of God. For only the Spirit of God can reveal what human reason cannot comprehend. The mystery of love is not something to be solved, but to be known through communion with its Source.

As you turn each page, may your heart be drawn nearer to the One who is both the Giver and the Gift.

May you come to see that love is not an idea, nor a feeling—but a Person.

And may this revelation change the way you see God, yourself, and every soul around you.

"He who does not love does not know God, for God is love."
— 1 John 4:8

CHAPTER ONE:
THE SOURCE OF LOVE —
GOD IS LOVE

"He who does not love does not know God, for God is love."
— 1 John 4:8

1. The Origin of Love

Before the first word of creation was ever spoken, love existed — not as an emotion, but as the eternal nature of God Himself. Love was not created; it is uncreated, because it is who God is. Every expression of His power, wisdom, and justice flows from that divine essence.

When we say "God is love," we are not describing what God does, but who He is. Love is not one of His attributes among many—it is the essence that gives life to them all. His holiness is loving holiness, His justice is loving justice, His power is loving power. Everything that proceeds from Him carries the mark of that divine love.

2. The Meaning of Love in the Scriptures

The word love appears hundreds of times in Scripture, but the depth of its meaning is often lost in translation. The Bible was written primarily in Hebrew (Old Testament) and Greek (New Testament), and both languages use different words to describe the kinds and expressions of love.

In Hebrew:

This is the most common Hebrew word for love. It comes from a root — (Ahavah) הָבְהַא.1 meaning "to give." True love, in the Hebrew understanding, is not based on what one receives, but on what one gives. This is why God's love is perfectly expressed in His giving:

 "For God so loved (ahav) the world that He gave His only begotten Son…"
— John 3:16
Ahavah shows us that love is an act of the will that flows.
from a heart of generosity

Often translated as lovingkindness, mercy, or steadfast love. This word — (Chesed) דָסֶח. 2 describes God's covenant love—the kind of love that remains faithful even when the other party fails. It is enduring, merciful, and loyal.

"Give thanks to the Lord, for He is good; His mercy (chesed) endures forever."
— Psalm 136:1
Chesed reveals the love that keeps covenant—a love.
rooted in grace and faithfulness

In Greek:

The Greek language, used in the New Testament, distinguishes several kinds of love, each revealing a different facet of God's heart.

1. Ἀγάπη (Agapē) — The highest and most divine form of love. It is unconditional, sacrificial, and self-giving. It seeks the good of others, even when there is no return. Agapē is the love of God for mankind, and it is the love believers are called to walk in.

   "Greater love (agapē) has no one than this, than to lay down one's life for his friends."
   — John 15:13

2. Φιλία (Philia) — This is brotherly love, the affection between friends or companions. It is mutual and warm, based on shared trust and companionship. Jesus demonstrated philia when He called His disciples friends.

   "You are My friends if you do whatever I command you."
   — John 15:14

3. Στοργή (Storgē) — Natural affection, such as the love within a family—parents for children, or siblings for one another. It speaks of deep, relational bonds. Paul used a form of this word when urging believers to love one another with brotherly affection (Romans 12:10).

4. Ἔρως (Eros) — Romantic or passionate love between a man and a woman. Though the word itself does not appear in the New Testament, the concept is part of God's creation order in marriage. Eros becomes holy when governed by agapē and directed by God's purpose.

3. The Layers of Divine Love

Each of these expressions of love, whether ahavah, chesed, or agapē, points to different ways God reveals Himself.

- In creation, His love gives.

- In covenant, His love remains.

- In Christ, His love redeems.

- In the Spirit, His love dwells within us.

Love, then, is not an abstract mystery—it is the revelation of the heart of God made visible.

"The love of God has been poured out in our hearts by the Holy Spirit who was given to us."
— Romans 5:5

4. The Eternal Fellowship of Love — Father, Son, and Holy Spirit

Before time began, before the foundation of the world was laid, before a single angelic song filled the heavens—God was love.

Love did not begin when man was created; it did not come into existence when God first spoke light into the darkness. Love was already there, existing within the eternal relationship of the Father, the Son, and the Holy Spirit.

This divine fellowship is the purest revelation of what love truly is—unity without rivalry, giving without measure, and communion without end.

The Father's Love for the Son

"For the Father loves the Son, and shows Him all things that He Himself does."
— John 5:20

The Father's love is the fountainhead of all love. Out of that love He gave the Son—not because He had to, but because love gives. This love is creative, generous, and overflowing. It was the love of the Father that conceived redemption long before man ever fell.

The Son's Love for the Father

"But that the world may know that I love the Father, and as the Father gave Me commandment, so I do."
— John 14:31

The Son's love is one of perfect obedience. Jesus' every word, miracle, and act of compassion flowed from His love for the Father. On the cross, His obedience was the ultimate expression of love: "Not My will, but Yours be done."

Love, therefore, is not proven by emotion, but by submission to the will of God.

The Spirit's Love — The Bond of Divine Unity

"The love of God has been poured out in our hearts by the Holy Spirit."
— Romans 5:5

The Holy Spirit is the living bond of love between the Father and the Son—the eternal flow of divine affection that unites them in perfect harmony. Through the Spirit, that same love now dwells in the hearts of believers, making us partakers of that heavenly fellowship.

This is the mystery of divine love: that what eternally existed within God Himself has now been shared with us through Christ.

5. The Expression of Love in Creation

When God said, "Let Us make man in Our image," it was not an act of mere power—it was an act of love. The "Us" in that declaration reveals divine relationship. God created man not out of need, but out of overflowing love, to reflect His image and share in His joy.

"The LORD has appeared of old to me, saying: 'Yes, I have loved you with an everlasting love; therefore with lovingkindness I have drawn you.'"
— Jeremiah 31:3

Every act of God from Genesis to Revelation is an expression of love's unfolding purpose. Even His judgments, though severe, are rooted in love—for His discipline is the expression of His desire to restore.

Creation itself testifies to love's abundance. The stars declare His glory, the oceans echo His depth, and every breath of life is a whisper of His affection.

6. The Mystery of Love Revealed in Redemption

The truest revelation of love, however, is seen not in creation, but in redemption.

When man fell, the love that formed him did not abandon him. Instead, love took on flesh, walked among the broken, and bore their sins upon the cross.

"But God demonstrates His own love toward us, in that while we were still sinners, Christ died for us."
— Romans 5:8

The cross is not just a symbol of suffering—it is the ultimate manifestation of divine love.

There, the Father gave, the Son obeyed, and the Spirit testified.

Love was not defeated; it triumphed.

The infinite God stooped down to embrace the unworthy, revealing that the highest power in the universe is not force, but love.

7. Conclusion — Love as the Essence of God

Everything begins and ends with love.

The Scriptures start with a Creator moved by love and end with a Bride united to her Beloved. From Genesis to Revelation, love is the golden thread that binds every promise, prophecy, and purpose together.

To know love is to know God.

To walk in love is to walk in His nature.

And to live by love is to reveal Him to the world.

"Beloved, let us love one another, for love is of God; and everyone who loves is born of God and knows God."
— 1 John 4:7

PRAYER AND REFLECTION

The Source of Love — "God Is Love"

Take a quiet moment to still your heart before the One who is Love itself. Let His Word speak to you personally.

Reflect:

Before creation, before sin, before your first breath — you were already known and loved. Love has always been God's plan for you. His heart has never changed, even when yours has wandered. Do you truly believe that? Have you allowed His love, not fear or guilt, to define your view of Him?

Ask yourself:

- Have I experienced God's love, or have I only heard about it?

- Do I see His commandments as heavy burdens, or as invitations to love?

- Have I received His love freely, or have I tried to earn it through works?

Let these questions draw you nearer to His heart.

A Prayer

Heavenly Father,

You are love itself — pure, holy, and unchanging. From the beginning You loved me, not because I was worthy, but because You are Love. I thank You for revealing Yourself through Your Word and through Your Son, Jesus Christ — the greatest expression of love the world has ever known.

Forgive me, Lord, for every time I have doubted Your love or failed to love others as You love me. Wash my heart clean from pride, fear, and selfishness. Draw me back into Your perfect fellowship — Father, Son, and Holy Spirit.

Lord Jesus, I receive You as the Gift of Love — the One who gave Himself for me. May Your love be shed abroad in my heart by the Holy Spirit, teaching me to love as You do: freely, faithfully, and sacrificially.

Transform me from within, that I may reflect Your love to the world around me.

Let my life become a testimony that God is love in Jesus' name.

Amen.

Scripture to Meditate On:

"Beloved, if God so loved us, we also ought to love one another."
— 1 John 4:11

CHAPTER TWO: LOVE CREATES — THE BREATH OF LIFE AND THE IMAGE OF GOD

"Then God said, 'Let Us make man in Our image, according to Our likeness; let them have dominion…' So God created man in His own image; in the image of God He created him; male and female He created them."
— Genesis 1:26–27, NKJV

1. Love Is the Reason for Creation

Everything that exists was born from the overflowing heart of Love.

Creation was not a necessity for God; it was a desire of Love to be expressed and shared. Love, by its very nature, cannot remain hidden—it longs to reveal itself, to give, to bring life.

Before time began, Love existed perfectly within the fellowship of the Father, the Son, and the Holy Spirit. Yet out of that perfect unity came a divine decision:

"Let Us make man in Our image..."

That statement was the first invitation ever spoken to humanity. It was Love saying, "Come, share in who We are."

Creation was not a display of power—it was a revelation of God's heart.

2. The Image and Likeness of God

To be made in the image and likeness of God (Hebrew: tselem and demuth) means far more than physical appearance. It speaks of spiritual resemblance, moral nature, and relational capacity.

God created humanity to reflect His character—to think, feel, and act in harmony with His divine essence. The greatest evidence of being in His image is the capacity to love.

When God breathed into Adam's nostrils "the breath of life" (Genesis 2:7, NKJV), it was not just oxygen that entered man—it was the Spirit of God, the spark of divine life that carries the imprint of Love.

In that moment, man became a living soul, capable of communion with his Creator.

To love, therefore, is to act according to the very purpose for which we were created. Every heartbeat was meant to echo the rhythm of divine affection.

3. The Breath of Life — Love Shared

The Hebrew phrase "nishmat chayyim" (נ.שֶׁמַ תַיֶּיח) literally means "the breath of lives." It implies not one, but a plurality of life—physical, spiritual, and eternal. When God breathed into Adam, He imparted not only biological life but also spiritual fellowship, the ability to love, to choose, and to reflect His glory.

That breath was Love Himself entering dust, transforming the lifeless into the living.

Thus, humanity was not created to exist independently of God, but to contain and express His life. The greatest tragedy of sin was not merely disobedience—it was separation from Love's breath.

Even today, every soul that comes to Christ experiences that same miracle anew. Through the Holy Spirit, the Breath of God once again fills the heart, restoring what was lost in Eden.

"And when He had said this, He breathed on them, and said to them, 'Receive the Holy Spirit.'"
— John 20:22, NKJV

4. Love's Authority and Responsibility

When God gave humanity dominion over creation, it was not a license for domination, but a call to stewardship in love.

To rule in God's image means to govern as He would—with compassion, righteousness, and humility. Every act of care, protection, and creativity reflects His nature.

But where love is absent, authority becomes abuse, and dominion becomes destruction. That is why the fall of man was not merely a moral failure—it was a fracture of the divine image within.

Love gives life, sin takes it.

Love restores, sin corrupts.

And yet, even in humanity's rebellion, Love did not withdraw. Instead, Love began its greatest work—the plan of redemption.

5. The Purpose of Creation — To Be Loved and To Love

Many people spend their lives searching for meaning, unaware that the answer was written into their very being: You were created to love and to be loved by God.

Love is not something God does occasionally; it is the reason you exist. Everything He has ever done—from forming the stars to shaping the heart—was motivated by love.

"The LORD has appeared of old to me, saying: 'Yes, I have loved you with an everlasting love; therefore with lovingkindness I have drawn you.'"
— Jeremiah 31:3, NKJV

That verse is the heartbeat of all creation.

Love desired you before you ever knew Him. Love drew you when you were far away. Love breathed life into you so that you might one day breathe it back in worship.

6. Conclusion — Love Is the Life of the Soul

Every soul without love is like a body without breath.

We may live, move, and accomplish much in the world, but without love, the essence of divine life is absent.

To be filled with the Spirit is to be filled with Love Himself—to live again by the same Breath that gave us life in the beginning. And when we walk in love, we become mirrors of the Creator, reflecting His light into the world around us.

"And we have known and believed the love that God has for us. God is love, and he who abides in love abides in God, and God in him."
— 1 John 4:16, NKJV

PRAYER AND REFLECTION

Love Creates — The Breath of Life and the Image of God

Reflect:

Pause and breathe deeply for a moment.

That breath you just took is not ordinary—it is evidence of Love's presence within you. From the dust of the ground, God breathed His own life into humanity. You are not an accident of nature, but a vessel of divine purpose.

God did not create you because He needed you; He created you because He loved you. Every heartbeat, every thought, and every gift within you carries the fingerprint of His love.

Yet, how often do we live unaware of this sacred truth?

How often do we search for meaning in creation while forgetting the Creator's embrace?

Ask yourself:

- Have I allowed God's love to define my worth?

- Do I see others as bearers of His image, worthy of love and dignity?

- Have I yielded every part of my life to the purpose for which I was created—to love and be loved by God?

Let these questions lead you into worship, not guilt. Let them draw you back to the Source of every breath.

A Prayer

Loving Father,

You are the breath of my life and the reason I exist. You formed me from the dust and filled me with Your Spirit. Thank You for loving me before I ever knew You, and for giving me the privilege to bear Your image.

Forgive me for the times I have forgotten my purpose, chasing the creation instead of the Creator. Breathe in me again, O Lord. Restore the life of Your Spirit within me. Let Your love flow through my heart as it did in the beginning.

Lord Jesus, I acknowledge You as the Living Word through whom all things were made. You are Love manifested in flesh. Teach me to live in Your likeness—to create peace where there is chaos, to give life where there is despair, and to love even when it costs me everything.

Holy Spirit, renew in me the breath of divine life. Fill me until Your love becomes my nature. May my words, thoughts, and actions reveal Your image to the world.

I surrender all that I am to the One who loved me first.

Breathe on me again, O Lord in Jesus' name.

Amen.

Scripture to Meditate On:

"And when He had said this, He breathed on them, and said to them, 'Receive the Holy Spirit.'"
— John 20:22, NKJV

CHAPTER THREE: LOVE BETRAYED — THE FALL AND THE LONGING OF GOD

"Then the LORD God called to Adam and said to him, 'Where are you?'"
— Genesis 3:9, NKJV

1. The Wound in Love's Heart

In the garden of Eden, love walked with man.

There was no fear, no shame, no distance—only perfect communion between the Creator and His creation. Every evening breeze carried the presence of God, and every moment was filled with peace.

But love, by its nature, allows freedom. For love that cannot be freely given is not love at all. God, in His wisdom, gave humanity the gift of choice—to love Him or to turn away.

When Adam and Eve reached for the forbidden fruit, they did more than disobey a command— they broke fellowship with Love itself.

Sin entered, and the pure bond between God and man was torn. The first sound that echoed after sin was not thunder or wrath, but the voice of a grieving Father:

"Where are you?"
— Genesis 3:9, NKJV

That cry was not one of anger but of love wounded—the voice of a Father searching for His lost children.

2. The Deception that Distorted Love

The serpent's strategy was subtle: he questioned God's love.

"Has God indeed said...?"
— Genesis 3:1, NKJV

By twisting God's word, Satan planted a seed of doubt in Eve's heart.

When the purity of love is questioned, obedience becomes difficult. Once love is distrusted, the heart becomes vulnerable to deception.

Eve saw the fruit, desired it, and took it—believing a lie that she could be like God without God. Adam followed, and love's image within man was darkened.

Sin is not merely breaking God's law; it is breaking His heart.

It is the rejection of love's truth and the embrace of self-centeredness— the opposite of all that God is.

3. The Shame and Separation

The moment sin entered, something divine departed.

Adam and Eve felt naked—not only physically, but spiritually. They had stepped out of the covering of love, and fear took its place.

"And they heard the sound of the LORD God walking in the garden... and Adam and his wife hid themselves from the presence of the LORD God."
— Genesis 3:8, NKJV

How tragic that the very presence that once brought joy now brought terror.

Sin distorts our perception of God—it makes the loving Father seem distant and severe. Yet even in their hiding, Love came seeking.

He clothed their shame with skins, a prophetic act pointing forward to the sacrifice of the Lamb. Even in judgment, mercy triumphed.

4. The Longing of God

From that moment, the story of Scripture became the story of God's pursuit.

Every covenant, every prophet, every act of grace flowed from the longing of a Father to restore what was lost.

God's heart is revealed again and again throughout the Bible:

"As I live," says the Lord GOD, "I have no pleasure in the death of the wicked, but that the wicked turn from his way and live."
— Ezekiel 33:11, NKJV

"How can I give you up, Ephraim? ... My heart churns within Me; My sympathy is stirred."
— Hosea 11:8, NK.IV

These are not the words of a distant deity but of a grieving Lover.

Though man turned away, Love refused to let go. God's justice demanded payment, but His mercy sought redemption. Thus began the unfolding mystery of salvation—the plan formed before the foundation of the world.

5. Love's Promise of Redemption

Even in Eden, God spoke a promise of hope:

"And I will put enmity between you and the woman, and between your seed and her Seed; He shall bruise your head, and you shall bruise His heel."
— Genesis 3:15, NKJV

This verse, often called the Protoevangelium (the first gospel), was love's declaration of war against sin and death.

Though man had fallen, Love had already prepared the way of return.

The Seed—Christ Himself—would one day come to crush the serpent's power and restore humanity to the heart of God.

The story of the Bible from that point forward is the story of this promise unfolding—Love chasing the lost through generations, covenants, and finally, the cross.

6. Conclusion — The God Who Still Calls

"Where are you?"

That question still echoes through the ages. It is the same call God makes to every wandering heart. He does not ask because He does not know where we are—He asks so that we might see where we have gone.

Love still seeks, still calls, still waits.

No matter how far one has fallen, His voice is the same—gentle, longing, and full of mercy.

The mystery of love is this: even when betrayed, Love does not stop loving.

18

"For I am persuaded that neither death nor life, nor angels nor principalities nor powers, nor things present nor things to come... shall be able to separate us from the love of God which is in Christ Jesus our Lord."
— Romans 8:38–39, NKJV

PRAYER AND REFLECTION

Love Betrayed — The Fall and the Longing of God

Reflect:

Close your eyes for a moment and imagine the garden — the stillness, the beauty, the peace. Then hear the voice of God breaking through the silence:

"Where are you?"
— Genesis 3:9, NKJV

That question is not one of condemnation but of longing. It is the voice of Love searching for the lost. From Eden until now, that voice has never stopped calling. It is the same voice that reaches through your guilt, your failures, your doubts, and whispers, "Come home."

The fall was not just Adam's story — it is ours.

Every time we choose our own way above God's, we repeat the garden's tragedy. Yet every time we repent, we step closer to Love's redeeming embrace.

God's heart still yearns for you — not because you are perfect, but because you are His.

Ask yourself:

- Have I hidden from God's love because of guilt or shame?

- Do I truly believe His love can restore what sin has broken?

- Am I ready to stop running and return to the One who calls me by name?

Let these reflections lead you into the arms of Love Himself.

A Prayer

Heavenly Father,

You are the God who still calls, even when I have wandered far. You are Love that refuses to give up on me. Today, I hear Your voice saying, "Where are you?" and I answer, "Here I am, Lord."

Forgive me for turning away from Your heart. Forgive me for trusting my own way instead of Yours. Cover my shame with Your mercy, just as You clothed Adam and Eve with compassion in the garden.

Lord Jesus, You are the promised Seed who crushed the serpent's head. Thank You for bearing my sin, my guilt, and my separation on the cross. Through You, I am reconciled, restored, and redeemed by Love.

Holy Spirit, breathe in me again the life of fellowship. Remove every fear that keeps me from running into the Father's arms. Teach me to live in Your love daily — to listen for Your voice, to walk in Your presence, and to reflect Your heart to others.

I return to You, Lord — not out of fear, but out of love.

Thank You for loving me even when I was unfaithful. Thank You for never stopping the search in Jesus' name Amen.

CHAPTER FOUR: LOVE PURSUES — COVENANTS, MERCY, AND REDEMPTION IN MOTION

"The LORD has appeared of old to me, saying: 'Yes, I have loved you with an everlasting love; therefore with lovingkindness I have drawn you.'"
— Jeremiah 31:3, NKJV

1. Love in Pursuit

From the moment Adam and Eve fell, Love began to pursue.

The cry "Where are you?" in the garden became the call of God through all generations. Though man hid, God kept seeking. Though sin increased, grace abounded. The flame of divine love never dimmed—it only burned brighter against the darkness.

The story of Scripture is not primarily about man searching for God, but God searching for man.

It is the story of covenants—sacred bonds of love by which God continually reached out to a fallen world. Each covenant revealed another layer of His mercy, unfolding His eternal plan of redemption until Love Himself came in flesh.

2. Love Preserves — The Covenant with Noah

After the flood, when the world had drowned in its own corruption, Love remembered mercy. God could have ended it all, but instead He made a promise.

"I establish My covenant with you: never again shall all flesh be cut off by the waters of the flood; never again shall there be a flood to destroy the earth."
— Genesis 9:11, NKJV

The rainbow became a sign of that covenant—a visible reminder that even when judgment comes, mercy follows.

Through Noah, God preserved life, proving that Love always seeks restoration, not destruction.

The rainbow still arcs across the sky as a testimony that Love keeps covenant. Even when humanity forgets, God remembers.

3. Love Calls — The Covenant with Abraham

When humanity again turned to idolatry, God found one man whose heart would believe.

He called Abram out of his homeland—not to make him a ruler, but to make him a vessel of blessing.

"I will make you a great nation; I will bless you and make your name great; and you shall be a blessing."
— Genesis 12:2, NKJV

Through Abraham, God revealed that His love is not confined by borders or bloodlines. This covenant was not merely about land or descendants—it was about the coming of a Redeemer through whom "all the families of the earth shall be blessed." (Genesis 12:3, NKJV)

Abraham's faith became the channel through which love would one day be fulfilled in Christ, the promised Seed.

"Now to Abraham and his Seed were the promises made… and to your Seed, who is Christ."
— Galatians 3:16, NKJV

Love calls us out of the familiar to walk by faith. Love always leads us from the seen to the unseen, from the known to the promise.

4. Love Redeems — The Covenant through Moses

Centuries later, Love pursued again—this time through a nation enslaved in Egypt. God heard the cries of His people and raised up Moses, not only to deliver them but to reveal His law of holiness.

"And I will take you as My people, and I will be your God."
— Exodus 6:7, NKJV

The covenant at Sinai was not a contract of performance but a covenant of relationship. God desired to dwell among His people, to walk with them once again. The tabernacle became the visible sign of His presence—a shadow of a greater reality to come.

Even when Israel broke the covenant, Love's heart broke with it. Through the prophets, God pleaded:

"Return, O backsliding children… for I am married to you."
— Jeremiah 3:14, NKJV

Divine love is not quick to anger nor slow to forgive. It corrects, it disciplines, but it never abandons.

5. Love Restores — The Promise of a New Covenant

Every covenant before Christ pointed to a greater one still to come—a covenant not written on tablets of stone, but on hearts of flesh.

"Behold, the days are coming, says the LORD, when I will make a new covenant... I will put My law in their minds, and write it on their hearts; and I will be their God, and they shall be My people."
— Jeremiah 31:31,33, NKJV

This was the heartbeat of Love—God preparing humanity for the day when His very Spirit would dwell within us. The sacrifices, the altars, the priesthood—all were prophetic shadows of the cross, where divine love and justice would finally meet.

The pursuit of God's love finds its climax in the person of Jesus Christ, the Mediator of the new covenant.

"But God demonstrates His own love toward us, in that while we were still sinners, Christ died for us."
— Romans 5:8, NKJV

6. Conclusion — The Covenant-Keeping God

Every promise God ever made was a step closer to Calvary.

From Noah's rainbow to Abraham's faith, from Moses' tablets to Jeremiah's prophecy—all were pieces of the same divine story: the relentless pursuit of Love for His lost creation.

God is not a distant ruler, but a covenant-keeping Father. He remembers mercy even when we forget Him. His love does not fail, because His Word cannot be broken.

"Know therefore that the LORD your God, He is God, the faithful God who keeps covenant and mercy for a thousand generations with those who love Him and keep His commandments."
— Deuteronomy 7:9, NKJV

PRAYER AND REFLECTION

Love Pursues — Covenants, Mercy, and Redemption in Motion

Reflect:

From Eden's garden to Calvary's cross, one truth remains unshaken: God never stopped pursuing. Every covenant, every promise, and every act of mercy reveals His unrelenting love.

Think of Noah — saved by grace when the world drowned in corruption.

Think of Abraham — called out of his comfort to become a vessel of blessing.

Think of Israel — delivered from slavery to be God's treasured people.

Through every generation, God's heart has whispered the same invitation:

"I will be your God, and you shall be My people."

Love does not give up; it waits. Love does not grow weary; it calls again and again.

And in the fullness of time, Love came down — not in thunder, but in the form of a Servant, to seal the everlasting covenant with His own blood.

Ask yourself:

- Have I recognized how God has pursued me personally through seasons of my life?

- Have I responded to His covenant invitation, or have I turned away in fear or pride?

- Do I live daily as one loved, chosen, and redeemed by the blood of the New Covenant?

Let your heart return to the God who has never stopped drawing you with lovingkindness.

A Prayer

Covenant-Keeping Father,

From the beginning, You have pursued me with everlasting love. You have remembered mercy when I deserved judgment, and You have called me by name when I was far from You. Thank You for the covenants of promise that reveal Your faithful heart.

Forgive me, Lord, for the times I have taken Your mercy for granted. Forgive me for when I have broken fellowship and forgotten that You desire relationship more than ritual. Draw me back to You, O Lord, for You are my portion forever.

Lord Jesus, You are the fulfillment of every covenant—the Lamb who sealed the promise with Your own blood. Through You, I have peace with the Father, forgiveness of sin, and the indwelling of the Holy Spirit. Teach me to live in the joy of this new covenant every day, walking in obedience and gratitude.

Holy Spirit, help me to keep covenant with my words, my heart, and my life. Let Your mercy flow through me, that I may become an instrument of reconciliation to others.

Thank You, Father, for pursuing me with unfailing love and for never giving up on me.

I renew my covenant with You today—willingly, joyfully, and completely.

In Jesus' name. Amen.

Scripture to Meditate On:

"Know therefore that the LORD your God, He is God, the faithful God who keeps covenant and mercy for a thousand generations with those who love Him and keep His commandments."
— Deuteronomy 7:9, NKJV

CHAPTER FIVE:
LOVE CAME DOWN —
THE INCARNATION OF
CHRIST

"And the Word became flesh and dwelt among us, and we beheld His glory, the glory as of the only begotten of the Father, full of grace and truth."
—John 1:14, NKJV

1. The Fulfillment of Love's Promise

For generations, prophets spoke of a coming Redeemer.

Isaiah foretold a virgin who would bear a Son.

Micah named the small town where He would be born.

Even the angelic hosts waited for the moment when heaven's greatest mystery would be unveiled —when Love would become visible.

All the covenants of old found their fulfillment in this one divine act:

God Himself stepped into human history.

The invisible became visible. The eternal entered time. The Creator walked among His creation.

"Behold, the virgin shall conceive and bear a Son, and shall call His name Immanuel."
— Isaiah 7:14, NKJV

"Which is translated, 'God with us.'"
— Matthew 1:23, NKJV

Love did not send a messenger this time—Love came in person.

2. The Humility of Love

When the King of Glory entered the world, He did not come clothed in splendor or born in a palace.

He came in weakness, wrapped in swaddling cloths, and laid in a manger.

"For you know the grace of our Lord Jesus Christ, that though He was rich, yet for your sakes He became poor, that you through His poverty might become rich."
— 2 Corinthians 8:9, NKJV

The humility of Jesus reveals the true character of divine love.

Love does not seek to be served, but to serve.

Love does not exalt itself, but humbles itself for the sake of others.

Every cry of the infant Christ was a declaration that God had come near—not in power to destroy, but in tenderness to redeem.

The Creator was now dependent upon His creation; the Sustainer of all things was held in a mother's arms.

This is the mystery of divine love—that the infinite God would limit Himself to save the finite.

3. The Manifestation of God's Nature

Jesus was not merely a messenger from God—He was God revealed.

Every word He spoke, every miracle He performed, every tear He shed revealed the heart of the Father.

"He who has seen Me has seen the Father."
— John 14:9, NKJV

In Jesus, love became tangible. The compassion that moved Him to touch lepers, to feed the hungry, to forgive the sinful, and to restore the broken was not human kindness alone—it was the very love of God made flesh.

The Incarnation was heaven's greatest declaration:

"I love you this much."

The manger led to the cross, and both were built from the same wood—love's obedience.

4. The Obedience of Love

The birth of Christ was the beginning of love's greatest mission—the road to redemption.

Every step He took on earth was guided by one motive: obedience to the Father's will.

"Then I said, 'Behold, I have come—In the volume of the book it is written of Me—To do Your will, O God.'"
— Hebrews 10:7, NKJV

Love is not proven in words but in obedience.

The Son of God left the glory of heaven not because He had to, but because He wanted to—for love's sake.

He came to fulfill what no human could, to live a perfect life under the law, and to offer Himself as the spotless Lamb of God.

5. The Nearness of Love

The Incarnation means that God is not far away.

He is not distant, detached, or unreachable.

Through Jesus, God walked where we walk, felt what we feel, and suffered what we suffer.

"For we do not have a High Priest who cannot sympathize with our weaknesses, but was in all points tempted as we are, yet without sin." — Hebrews 4:15, NKJV

This is love in its most personal form—God with us.

He did not just visit humanity; He became one of us so that we could one day be one with Him.

6. Conclusion — Love Revealed in Flesh

From eternity, Love longed to be known.

Through creation, Love was expressed.

Through the covenants, Love was promised.

But through the Incarnation, Love was revealed.

Jesus Christ is not simply the bearer of God's love—He is that love.

To look upon Him is to see the full radiance of divine compassion, grace, truth, and glory.

"For it pleased the Father that in Him all the fullness should dwell."
— Colossians 1:19, NKJV

In Bethlehem, heaven kissed the earth—and that kiss still echoes in the hearts of all who receive Him.

PRAYER AND REFLECTION

Love Came Down — The Incarnation of Christ

Reflect:

Close your eyes and imagine that holy night in Bethlehem.

The world was silent, yet heaven rejoiced. The Word became flesh, and Love took His first breath among men.

There in that humble manger, the Creator became the created. The One who spoke galaxies into existence now cried as a child. Every breath He took declared the same message: "I have come for you."

How incredible that the infinite God would step into time, into weakness, into poverty — all to reveal His heart.

This is love in its purest form: not distant, not abstract, but personal and present.

Ask yourself:

- Have I truly received the reality that God loves me enough to come near?

- Do I see Jesus not just as Savior, but as Emmanuel — "God with us"?

- Does His humility inspire me to love and serve others the same way?

Let the wonder of His coming fill your heart again with gratitude, reverence, and love.

A Prayer

Heavenly Father,

I stand in awe of Your love that came down. You wrapped eternity in humanity so that I could know You. You sent Your Son, not in majesty, but in humility — the Word made flesh, full of grace and truth. Thank You for not leaving us in darkness, but for bringing the light of Your presence into our world.

Lord Jesus, You are Emmanuel — God with us. You stepped into my brokenness, felt my pain, and bore my sin. You are the perfect revelation of the Father's heart. Thank You for loving me so deeply that You were willing to become like me, so that I could become like You.

Forgive me for the times I have taken Your coming for granted or allowed the noise of the world to drown out the wonder of Your presence. Teach me to walk daily in the awareness that You are near — not only in history, but in my heart.

Holy Spirit, awaken in me the same humility and obedience that filled Christ. Let His love transform my thoughts, my words, and my actions. Help me to reflect His light to those still walking in darkness.

Thank You, Lord, for the gift of Your Son — the greatest expression of love ever given.

I worship You, my King, my Savior, my Emmanuel.

In Jesus' name. Amen.

Scripture to Meditate On:

"And the Word became flesh and dwelt among us, and we beheld His glory, the glory as of the only begotten of the Father, full of grace and truth."
— John 1:14, NKJV

CHAPTER SIX:
LOVE OBEYED — THE CROSS, THE COST, AND THE VICTORY

"And being found in appearance as a man, He humbled Himself and became obedient to the point of death, even the death of the cross."
— Philippians 2:8, NKJV

1. The Depth of Obedient Love

Love is not proven in words, but in obedience.

From the cradle to the cross, every step Jesus took was a step of love's surrender.

He came not to do His own will, but the will of the Father who sent Him.

"Then I said, 'Behold, I have come—In the volume of the book it is written of Me—To do Your will, O God.'"
— Hebrews 10:7, NKJV

The cross was not a tragedy; it was the triumph of obedience.

Through the suffering of the Son, Love revealed its full measure — not seeking its own, but giving itself completely for the salvation of others.

Every nail, every thorn, every drop of blood was the language of perfect love speaking to a fallen world:

"I am willing."

2. The Garden of Surrender

Before the cross came Gethsemane.

In that dark and lonely garden, Love wrestled with the weight of humanity's sin.

There, Jesus fell to the ground, overwhelmed with sorrow, and prayed:

"O My Father, if it is possible, let this cup pass from Me; nevertheless, not as I will, but as You will."
— Matthew 26:39, NKJV

Those words define true love — a heart that chooses the Father's will above its own comfort.

The agony of the cross began long before the nails; it began when Love chose obedience in the face of suffering.

Gethsemane was love tested.

Calvary was love proven.

3. The Cross — The Cost of Love

The cross stands at the center of history because it stands at the center of God's heart.

There, divine justice met divine mercy. There, wrath and grace embraced.

Love bore the curse so that we might receive the blessing.

"He Himself bore our sins in His own body on the tree, that we, having died to sins, might live for righteousness—by whose stripes you were healed."
— 1 Peter 2:24, NKJV

Jesus did not die as a victim, but as a Victor.

He was not overcome by evil — He overcame evil with good.

The cross is not a symbol of defeat, but of divine love's greatest victory.

Sin was conquered.

Satan was disarmed.

The veil was torn.

And humanity was invited back into the presence of God.

4. The Power of Perfect Obedience

Through one act of disobedience, Adam brought death.

Through one act of perfect obedience, Christ brought life.

"For as by one man's disobedience many were made sinners, so also by one Man's obedience many will be made righteous."
— Romans 5:19, NKJV

The obedience of Jesus was not reluctant—it was joyful, born from love.

True obedience flows not from fear, but from devotion.

Love transforms command into desire, duty into delight.

Every believer who follows Christ walks the same path of love's obedience—carrying the cross daily, surrendering self-will, and trusting the Father's plan.

It is costly, but it is the only path that leads to glory.

5. The Victory of Love

When Jesus cried, "It is finished!" (John 19:30, NKJV), He declared the end of sin's reign and the beginning of redemption's dawn.

That cry was not of defeat but of fulfillment—Love had accomplished its mission.

The cross was the battlefield where Heaven triumphed over Hell.

The blood that fell to the ground broke the curse that bound humanity.

Through that sacrifice, the chains of death were shattered, and the gates of grace were opened to all who believe.

"Having disarmed principalities and powers, He made a public spectacle of them, triumphing over them in it."
— Colossians 2:15, NKJV

Love's obedience did not end in suffering—it ended in victory.

And because of that victory, every believer can now stand forgiven, free, and filled with the Spirit of Love.

6. Conclusion — The Glory Beyond the Cost

The cross teaches us this eternal truth:

Obedience that costs nothing changes nothing.

But obedience born of love changes everything.

Jesus' obedience changed the course of human destiny.

He endured the cross, despising the shame, because of the joy set before Him—the joy of seeing you and me reconciled to God.

"Therefore God also has highly exalted Him and given Him the name which is above every name."
— Philippians 2:9, NKJV

The suffering of Love was not the end—it was the doorway to glory.

And the same is true for all who follow Him: the cost of obedience is great, but the glory to be revealed is far greater.

PRAYER AND REFLECTION

Love Obeyed — The Cross, the Cost, and the Victory

Reflect:

The cross is not merely a symbol of suffering — it is the revelation of love's ultimate obedience.

Every drop of blood that fell from Jesus' body spoke one truth: Love obeys, even when it costs everything.

Take a moment to imagine yourself at Calvary.

See the Lamb of God hanging there — bruised, bleeding, yet victorious.

Hear Him whisper, "It is finished." And realize — it was for you.

He obeyed because He loved.

He endured because He saw beyond the pain to the glory of redemption — your salvation, your freedom, your reconciliation.

Ask yourself:

- Have I embraced the cost of obedience, or have I avoided the cross in my own walk with God?

- Do I obey the Lord out of fear, or out of love?

- Have I allowed the victory of the Cross to transform my heart and set me free from sin's power?

Let the obedience of Jesus awaken in you a fresh desire to love and obey God from the depths of your heart.

A Prayer

Heavenly Father,

Thank You for the gift of Your Son — the perfect example of love's obedience. In Him, I see Your heart revealed: a love that serves, suffers, and saves. Thank You for sending Jesus to bear my sin, my shame, and my punishment on the cross.

Lord Jesus, You obeyed even to the point of death, and through that obedience, You triumphed over sin and death. I kneel before Your cross today with gratitude and reverence. Forgive me for every time I have chosen comfort over obedience, and my will over Yours.

Teach me, Lord, to walk in the same obedience that marked Your life — not out of fear, but out of love. Give me the courage to carry my cross daily and follow You, knowing that true victory comes through surrender.

Holy Spirit, strengthen me when obedience feels difficult. Remind me of the joy that comes after the cost, and of the glory that awaits those who endure in love. Let the power of the Cross live in me — cleansing my heart, transforming my mind, and filling me with holy passion to do the Father's will.

I give myself completely to You, Lord.

May my life echo the same words of my Savior:

"Not my will, but Yours be done." In Jesus' name. Amen.

Scripture to Meditate On:

"And being found in appearance as a man, He humbled Himself and became obedient to the point of death, even the death of the cross."
— Philippians 2:8, NKJV

CHAPTER SEVEN: LOVE POURED OUT — THE SPIRIT AND THE BIRTH OF THE CHURCH

"Now hope does not disappoint, because the love of God has been poured out in our hearts by the Holy Spirit who was given to us."
— Romans 5:5, NKJV

1. Love Does Not End at the Cross

The Cross was not the conclusion of love's story — it was the beginning of a new chapter.

When Jesus declared, "It is finished," He was not saying that love had ended, but that the work of redemption was complete. Now, the very love that conquered death was ready to be poured out into those who would believe.

Love came down in Bethlehem, obeyed at Calvary, and on the day of Pentecost, Love came to dwell within.

Through the Holy Spirit, the presence of Christ — once limited to one body — was multiplied in countless hearts around the world.

2. The Promise of the Father

Before His ascension, Jesus made a promise to His disciples:

"And behold, I send the Promise of My Father upon you; but tarry in the city of Jerusalem until you are endued with power from on high."
— Luke 24:49, NKJV

That promise was not merely about power for ministry, but power to love as God loves.

For three years, the disciples had walked beside Love Himself, yet even they could not fully love until Love filled them from within.

Jesus knew that to continue His work, they needed more than instruction — they needed infusion.

They needed the same Spirit that moved in Him to move in them.

3. The Day Love Filled the Earth

"When the Day of Pentecost had fully come, they were all with one accord in one place."
— Acts 2:1, NKJV

In that upper room, 120 believers waited — not with knowledge, but with hunger.

Suddenly, the sound of a rushing mighty wind filled the house, and tongues of fire rested upon them. The Holy Spirit came — not as a guest, but as a Resident.

The promise was fulfilled:

"I will pour out My Spirit on all flesh."
— Joel 2:28, NKJV

In that moment, heaven touched earth again.

Love, once crucified, now lived inside His people.

The Church was born — not through ritual or tradition, but through the outpouring of divine love.

Every word they spoke, every miracle they performed, every soul they reached flowed from that inner river of Love.

4. The Fellowship of Love

The early Church was not built by organization but by love in action.

They shared their possessions, prayed together, broke bread together, and worshiped in unity of heart.

"Now all who believed were together, and had all things in common."
— Acts 2:44, NKJV

This was not human generosity — it was the overflow of divine love.

The same Spirit that united the Father and the Son now united believers into one body.

Through the Spirit, the Church became the visible expression of Christ's love on earth.

Love no longer walked in one body — it walked in many.

5. The Mission of Love

Jesus said:

"As the Father has sent Me, I also send you."
— John 20:21, NKJV

The mission of the Church is the continuation of Christ's mission — to reveal the heart of the Father to a dying world.

But this mission cannot be fulfilled by human strength alone; it requires the life of the Spirit within.

The Holy Spirit is not given to make us feel spiritual, but to make us live sacrificially.

He empowers us to love the unlovable, forgive the unforgivable, and reach the unreachable.

Wherever the Spirit moves, love moves.

Wherever the Spirit dwells, grace abounds.

Wherever the Spirit speaks, hearts are healed.

6. Love as the Mark of the Church

The true evidence of the Spirit is not gifts alone — it is love.

Paul wrote:

"Though I speak with the tongues of men and of angels, but have not love, I have become sounding brass or a clanging cymbal."
— 1 Corinthians 13:1, NKJV

Without love, even the most powerful ministry is empty.

Love is the fragrance that identifies the Church as belonging to Christ.

The world will not know us by our buildings or doctrines, but by our love for one another.

"By this all will know that you are My disciples, if you have love for one another."
— John 13:35, NKJV

Love poured out through the Spirit transforms the Church from an institution into a living organism — the very heartbeat of Christ on earth.

7. Conclusion — The Spirit, the Fire, and the Flow of Love

The Holy Spirit is the continuing presence of Jesus on earth.

He is the fire that burns within every believer and the river that flows through every surrendered life.

Love did not remain on the cross; Love now lives in you.

Every time you forgive, every time you serve, every time you give, every time you pray — Love moves again through your life.

"The Spirit and the bride say, 'Come!'"
— Revelation 22:17, NKJV

The story of love that began before time now continues through the Church — the Bride of Christ, filled with the Spirit, awaiting the return of her Beloved.

PRAYER AND REFLECTION

Love Poured Out — The Spirit and the Birth of the Church

Reflect:

The same Spirit who hovered over the waters in creation, who filled the prophets, and who raised Jesus from the dead now longs to fill you.

You were never meant to live the Christian life by human strength. You were created to be a temple of Love Himself.

The Holy Spirit is not a distant force — He is the presence of the Father and the Son dwelling in your heart.

He comforts, convicts, empowers, and transforms. He pours out the very love of God within you, teaching you to love beyond what is humanly possible.

Ask yourself:

- Have I allowed the Holy Spirit to fill every part of my life?

- Do I walk in the power of love, or am I trying to serve God in my own strength?

- Is my life a channel through which God's love flows to others?

Take a moment to open your heart — not partially, but fully — and invite the Holy Spirit to fill you afresh.

Let the same love that moved through Christ now move through you.

A Prayer

Heavenly Father,

Thank You for not leaving us comfortless but for sending the Holy Spirit, the Spirit of truth, to dwell within us. Thank You for pouring out Your love into my heart through Him. You have not called me to serve You by my strength, but by Your Spirit.

Lord Jesus, You are the risen Love who breathes new life into Your Church. Thank You for baptizing me in the Holy Spirit and fire, for calling me to be Your witness, and for filling me with power to love as You love. Teach me to abide in You daily, and to let Your love flow freely through my words and actions.

Holy Spirit, I welcome You.

Fill every part of my being — my heart, my mind, my will. Burn away all fear, pride, and selfishness. Let Your fire refine me and Your presence overflow through me.

Make me a vessel of Your compassion, a light in darkness, and a voice of truth in a hurting world.

Unite me with Your Church, Lord, in love and purpose. May we walk in the power of the Spirit, revealing Jesus to all who are lost and weary.

Thank You for the outpouring of Your love.

Thank You that heaven now lives within me.

I am Yours forever.

In Jesus' name. Amen.

Scripture to Meditate On:

"Now hope does not disappoint, because the love of God has been poured out in our hearts by the Holy Spirit who was given to us."
— Romans 5:5, NKJV

CHAPTER EIGHT: LOVE PERFECTED — THE FRUITS OF THE SPIRIT AND TRUE FELLOWSHIP

"My little children, let us not love in word or in tongue, but in deed and in truth."
— 1 John 3:18, NKJV

"But the fruit of the Spirit is love, joy, peace, longsuffering, kindness, goodness, faithfulness, gentleness, self-control. Against such there is no law."
— Galatians 5:22–23, NKJV

1. Love Maturing Within

When the Holy Spirit fills the believer, He plants a divine seed — the seed of love.

But like every seed, it must grow, be nurtured, and come to maturity.

Love is perfected not through ease, but through endurance.

It deepens in prayer, matures through obedience, and shines brightest in trial.

To be filled with the Spirit is the beginning; to walk in the Spirit is the journey; to bear the fruit of the Spirit is the evidence.

"He who abides in love abides in God, and God in him. Love has been perfected among us in this…"
— 1 John 4:16–17, NKJV

Love perfected means love that has come full circle — from God, through us, back to God again.

2. The First Fruit — Love

Paul lists nine fruits of the Spirit, but love stands first because it is the root from which all others grow.

Joy springs from love rejoicing in God.

Peace flows from love resting in His will.

Patience waits because love endures.

Kindness acts because love gives.

Faithfulness stands because love remains.

Gentleness forgives because love humbles itself.

Self-control resists because love honors God above desire.

Every fruit of the Spirit is love in a different expression — love rejoicing, love enduring, love giving, love forgiving.

"And above all these things put on love, which is the bond of perfection."
— Colossians 3:14, NKJV

3. The Fellowship of Love

The true Church is not united by denomination, language, or tradition — it is united by the Spirit of Love.

The early believers were of "one heart and one soul" because they shared one Spirit and one love.

"By this all will know that you are My disciples, if you have love for one another."
— John 13:35, NKJV

Fellowship without love is empty religion.

But when love governs the heart, even the simplest gathering becomes a dwelling place of God's presence.

Love does not compete — it completes.

It builds bridges, not walls.

It seeks restoration, not revenge.

True fellowship is not about sameness but about oneness in Christ.

"Be kindly affectionate to one another with brotherly love, in honor giving preference to one another."
— Romans 12:10, NKJV

4. The Testing of Love

Love cannot be perfected without being tested.

Trials reveal what words cannot.

When we are wronged, love forgives.

When we are overlooked, love still serves.

When we are wounded, love heals instead of retaliating.

"Beloved, do not think it strange concerning the fiery trial which is to try you..."
— 1 Peter 4:12, NKJV

God does not test us to destroy us, but to deepen us — to refine our hearts until His love becomes our natural response.

It is in these refining fires that love moves from emotion to revelation, from words to action.

5. The Goal of Love — Christ Formed in Us

The work of the Holy Spirit is to form Christ within the believer.

Every fruit of the Spirit is a reflection of His nature.

As love matures, we begin to see less of self and more of Him.

"My little children, for whom I labor in birth again until Christ is formed in you."
— Galatians 4:19, NKJV

This is the goal of every believer — that the life of Christ would be visible through us.

Love perfected is Christ reproduced in human hearts — the invisible God seen again through visible lives.

When love rules, fear fades, pride dies, and grace reigns.

It is not our gifts that prove we know Him — it is our love that reveals we belong to Him.

6. Conclusion — The Circle of Love Complete

Love began in the heart of God, was revealed through the Son, poured out by the Spirit, and is now perfected in us.

It is the eternal circle of divine fellowship — the Father loving through the Son, the Son loving through the Spirit, and the Spirit loving through us.

"If we love one another, God abides in us, and His love has been perfected in us."
— 1 John 4:12, NKJV

Love perfected is heaven touching earth — God's character fully alive in human hearts.

And when that happens, the world sees Jesus again.

PRAYER AND REFLECTION

Love Perfected — The Fruits of the Spirit and True Fellowship

Reflect:

When the Holy Spirit comes to dwell within us, He plants the seed of divine love. Yet, like every living seed, that love must grow, be nurtured, and bear fruit.

Love perfected is not about perfection without weakness; it is about maturity — love that endures through trials, forgives when wronged, and keeps giving even when it costs something. It is love that no longer depends on emotion but flows from revelation.

God's desire is not only to fill us with love but to form us into love. The fruit of the Spirit is the visible evidence that we have been transformed from within.

Ask yourself:

- Is the love of God growing and maturing in me daily?

- Do others see Christ's nature in how I speak, serve, and forgive?

- Am I walking in fellowship that reflects the love of the Father, the Son, and the Holy Spirit?

Let your heart yield again to the gentle work of the Spirit. Let Him perfect in you what He has begun.

A Prayer

Heavenly Father,

Thank You for planting Your love within my heart through the Holy Spirit. I am humbled that You would make me a dwelling place for Your presence. I ask You to perfect Your love in me, to make me more like Jesus day by day.

Lord Jesus, You are love made visible. You showed what love looks like in word and deed — patient, gentle, forgiving, and steadfast. Help me to follow Your example and to walk in Your steps. Let Your love be the foundation of all I do.

Holy Spirit, cultivate the fruit of love in me. Remove every root of bitterness, pride, or selfishness that hinders Your work. Let joy, peace, kindness, faithfulness, and self-control grow from the soil of my heart. Shape my character until Christ is fully formed within me.

Teach me to love not only in words, but in truth and in action. Strengthen me to forgive quickly, serve willingly, and live humbly. May my life bear fruit that glorifies my Father in heaven.

Perfect Your love in me, Lord, until my heart beats in rhythm with Yours.

Let others see Jesus through the way I love.

In Jesus' name. Amen.

Scripture to Meditate On:

"If we love one another, God abides in us, and His love has been perfected in us."
— 1 John 4:12, NKJV

CHAPTER NINE: LOVE IN SUFFERING — THE REFINING OF THE HEART

"Beloved, do not think it strange concerning the fiery trial which is to try you, as though some strange thing happened to you; but rejoice to the extent that you partake of Christ's sufferings, that when His glory is revealed, you may also be glad with exceeding joy."
— 1 Peter 4:12–13, NKJV

1. Love Tested by Fire

The truest measure of love is not found in comfort but in suffering.

It is easy to love when life is kind, but real love endures the fire. It holds on when everything else is stripped away.

When God allows His children to walk through trials, He is not punishing them—He is refining them.

The furnace of affliction does not consume love; it purifies it.

"But He knows the way that I take; when He has tested me, I shall come forth as gold."
— Job 23:10, NKJV

Every trial removes another layer of self, pride, and fear until only the gold of pure love remains.

The same fire that destroys the counterfeit strengthens the genuine.

2. The Example of Christ's Suffering

Jesus, the Son of Love, was also the Man of Sorrows.

He knew rejection, betrayal, and pain—yet never stopped loving.

On the cross, as nails pierced His flesh, love spoke its purest words:

"Father, forgive them, for they do not know what they do."
— Luke 23:34, NKJV

That is the power of divine love—it suffers without resentment and gives without measure.

Every drop of blood was love enduring, forgiving, and redeeming.

If Christ's love could not be quenched by suffering, then neither should ours.

He showed us that love does not retreat in pain—it overcomes through it.

"Greater love has no one than this, than to lay down one's life for his friends."
— John 15:13, NKJV

3. The Purpose of Pain

Pain, in the hands of God, becomes an instrument of transformation.

Suffering peels away the illusions of self-sufficiency, bringing us back to total dependence on the Father's love.

It is often in the darkest nights that we see the brightest stars.

In weakness, we discover strength; in loss, we find what truly lasts.

Suffering reveals what is real—it exposes our heart and purifies our motives.

"My brethren, count it all joy when you fall into various trials, knowing that the testing of your faith produces patience."
— James 1:2–3, NKJV

Love refined in suffering becomes unshakable because it no longer depends on circumstances.

It learns to rest in God, not in outcomes.

4. The Fellowship of His Sufferings

Paul wrote that he longed to "know Him and the power of His resurrection, and the fellowship of His sufferings." (Philippians 3:10, NKJV)

To share in Christ's suffering is to share in His heart — to feel what He feels, to weep as He wept, to love as He loved.

This fellowship is not something to be feared but cherished, for it draws us deeper into intimacy with the One who first loved us.

Through pain, we come to understand His compassion.

Through trials, we touch His endurance.

Through rejection, we learn His mercy.

Suffering becomes the classroom where love learns the language of heaven.

5. Love That Endures

The world's love fades when it is wounded, but God's love grows stronger in adversity.

When love endures suffering, it testifies to the world that it is not human—it is divine.

"Love suffers long and is kind... bears all things, believes all things, hopes all things, endures all things. Love never fails."
— 1 Corinthians 13:4, 7–8, NKJV

True love cannot fail because its source cannot fail.

When we suffer in love for Christ or for others, we share in His nature.

That kind of love cannot be destroyed—it only deepens.

6. The Glory After the Pain

The story of love does not end in suffering—it ends in glory.

Every tear shed in faith becomes a seed of future joy.

Every wound becomes a doorway to greater revelation.

"For our light affliction, which is but for a moment, is working for us a far more exceeding and eternal weight of glory."
— 2 Corinthians 4:17, NKJV

Heaven keeps a record of every tear, and none are wasted.

In eternity, love's endurance will shine brighter than any crown.

The fire that once burned will be remembered as the fire that refined.

7. Conclusion — The Beauty of Refined Love

Love that has never been tested remains shallow, but love that has endured suffering becomes eternal.

It is the kind of love that reflects the Lamb who was slain and yet reigns forever in glory.

When we allow God to refine us through pain, we become living testimonies that love is stronger than suffering.

It is the mystery of divine transformation — that what was meant to wound us becomes what makes us whole.

"We love Him because He first loved us."
— 1 John 4:19, NKJV

PRAYER AND REFLECTION

Love in Suffering — The Refining of the Heart

Reflect:

Suffering is never easy, yet within it lies a holy mystery: God refines what He loves. The fire that feels painful is often the very fire that purifies, shaping our hearts to mirror His own.

When you walk through the valley, remember — Love walks with you.

He does not stand at a distance; He carries you through.

The same God who allowed Joseph's pit, Job's testing, and Christ's cross is the same God who transforms pain into purpose and ashes into beauty.

Ask yourself:

- What has suffering revealed about my heart and my relationship with God?

- Have I allowed pain to harden me, or to soften me into His likeness?

- Do I see my trials as punishments, or as refining flames in the hands of perfect Love?

Let the Holy Spirit help you see your scars not as reminders of loss, but as testimonies of love's endurance.

A Prayer

Heavenly Father,

Thank You for Your steadfast love, even in times of pain. I confess that I do not always understand Your ways, but I trust Your heart. You are too wise to make mistakes and too loving to be unkind.

Lord Jesus, You are the Man of Sorrows who understands my suffering. You bore pain, rejection, and loss — yet never stopped loving. Teach me to walk in that same endurance, to love even when it hurts, and to forgive as You forgave.

Holy Spirit, refine my heart in the fire of Your holiness. Remove fear, bitterness, and pride. Let every trial draw me nearer to the Father's heart and shape me into the image of Christ. Give me grace to rejoice, knowing that suffering produces endurance, endurance produces character, and character produces hope.

When I cannot trace Your hand, help me to trust Your heart.

When I do not see the purpose, remind me that love is still at work.

May every tear I cry water the seeds of faith, and may every trial produce fruit that glorifies You.

Thank You, Lord, that pain is not the end — glory is.

I surrender my heart to be refined by Your love, until nothing remains but You.

In Jesus' name. Amen.

Scripture to Meditate On:

"For our light affliction, which is but for a moment, is working for us a far more exceeding and eternal weight of glory."
— *2 Corinthians 4:17, NKJV*

CHAPTER TEN:
LOVE'S TRIUMPH — THE BRIDE, THE LAMB, AND ETERNITY

"Let us be glad and rejoice and give Him glory, for the marriage of the Lamb has come, and His wife has made herself ready."
— Revelation 19:7, NKJV

1. The Final Victory of Love

From before creation to the final pages of Revelation, love has been the heartbeat of God's story.

It began in the Father's heart, was revealed through the Son, and perfected by the Spirit. And one day, this love will reach its eternal fulfillment when the Bride and the Lamb are united in glory.

Every promise, every covenant, every act of redemption points to this moment — the great wedding feast of eternity.

What began in Eden's garden will end in the garden of God, where the curse will be no more, and love will reign forever.

"And I heard, as it were, the voice of a great multitude… saying, 'Alleluia! For the Lord God Omnipotent reigns!'"
— Revelation 19:6, NKJV

2. The Bride Made Ready

The Church — the redeemed of the Lord — is called the Bride of Christ.

She has been chosen, cleansed, and prepared through the washing of the Word and the refining of the Spirit.

Every trial, every tear, every act of obedience has been part of her preparation.

"Christ also loved the church and gave Himself for her, that He might sanctify and cleanse her with the washing of water by the word."
— Ephesians 5:25–26, NKJV

The Bride's beauty is not outward but inward — a purity born of surrender, humility, and faithfulness. She is clothed in righteousness, adorned with grace, and radiant with love.

Her garments are not her own; they are the garments of the Lamb who redeemed her.

"And to her it was granted to be arrayed in fine linen, clean and bright, for the fine linen is the righteous acts of the saints."
— Revelation 19:8, NKJV

3. The Marriage of the Lamb

The marriage of the Lamb is not a metaphor — it is the culmination of divine love.

It is the moment when Christ, the Bridegroom, receives His Bride into eternal fellowship — where heaven and earth are joined in perfect union.

All the longing of the ages, all the waiting of creation, all the prayers of the saints find their answer here: Love at last fulfilled.

"And I heard a loud voice from heaven saying, 'Behold, the tabernacle of God is with men, and He will dwell with them, and they shall be His people.'"
— Revelation 21:3, NKJV

In that eternal embrace, there will be no more separation, no more pain, no more distance. Love will reign completely, forever unbroken, forever new.

4. The Joy of the Redeemed

Love's triumph will overflow in joy beyond description.

All of heaven will resound with praise, and every redeemed heart will sing the song of the Lamb:

"You are worthy... for You were slain, and have redeemed us to God by Your blood out of every tribe and tongue and people and nation."
— Revelation 5:9, NKJV

This joy is not temporary; it is eternal.

Every sorrow will be turned into rejoicing. Every wound will become a testimony. Every moment of faithfulness will echo through eternity.

The glory that awaits us is not just a place — it is a Person.

To see Him face to face, to behold the One who loved us and gave Himself for us — this is love's greatest reward.

"We shall see Him as He is."
— 1 John 3:2, NKJV

5. The Eternal Kingdom of Love

In the new heavens and new earth, love will be the atmosphere of eternity.

There will be no sin to stain, no sorrow to divide, no darkness to hide.

The Lamb will be the light, and His glory will fill all things.

"And there shall be no more curse, but the throne of God and of the Lamb shall be in it, and His servants shall serve Him."
— Revelation 22:3, NKJV

The eternal purpose of God will be fully unveiled — to dwell among a people transformed by His love, forever united with Him in perfect communion.

Love will never again be betrayed or resisted. It will reign as the law, the language, and the life of the Kingdom of God.

6. Conclusion — The Mystery Complete

The mystery of love that began before time will find its completion in eternity.

The Lamb who was slain will stand in glory, and His Bride will stand beside Him — not as a servant, but as a beloved partner in His everlasting reign.

Every tear, every trial, every act of obedience will be remembered as a step in love's story — a story that ends not in sorrow, but in everlasting joy.

"Now abide faith, hope, love, these three; but the greatest of these is love."
— 1 Corinthians 13:13, NKJV

The story of God begins and ends with love — and those who live in love will live in God forever

PRAYER AND REFLECTION

Love's Triumph — The Bride, the Lamb, and Eternity

Reflect:

From the beginning of creation, God's desire has been relationship.

Love sought Adam in the garden, pursued Israel through covenant, revealed itself in Christ, and now prepares the Church as His Bride.

This is love's final triumph — the moment when every scar becomes beauty, every tear becomes joy, and every promise is fulfilled in the presence of the Lamb.

He is not a distant God waiting for us from afar — He is a Bridegroom longing for His Bride.

Ask yourself:

- Am I living in expectation of that glorious day when I will see Jesus face to face?

- Have I kept my heart pure and ready, clothed in righteousness and faith?

- Does my life reflect the love and devotion of a Bride preparing for her Bridegroom?

Let this truth awaken a deeper longing in your heart for Christ's return — and let that longing shape how you live today.

A Prayer

Heavenly Father,

Your love is eternal, unchanging, and victorious. From the beginning, You desired a people who would dwell in Your presence forever. Thank You for redeeming me through the blood of the Lamb and making me part of the Bride of Christ.

Lord Jesus, You are the Bridegroom of my soul — the One who loved me and gave Yourself for me. I long for the day when I will see You face to face, when faith will become sight and love will be perfected in Your glory. Prepare my heart, Lord. Cleanse me from every stain and clothe me in the garments of righteousness, that I may be ready for Your coming.

Holy Spirit, keep my lamp burning bright. Fill me with oil—the love, faith, and holiness that sustain me in this waiting hour. Teach me to live as one who belongs to heaven, even while I walk upon the earth. Let my life bear witness to the hope of Your return and the beauty of Your Bride.

Thank You, Lord, for including me in Your eternal story of love.

May my heart remain faithful until the day the trumpet sounds and I hear the Bridegroom's call: "Come, My beloved."

I worship You, my Redeemer, my King, my Eternal Love.

In Jesus' name. Amen.

Scripture to Meditate On:

"And I heard a loud voice from heaven saying, 'Behold, the tabernacle of God is with men, and He will dwell with them, and they shall be His people. God Himself will be with them and be their God.'"
— Revelation 21:3, NKJV

CHAPTER ELEVEN: THE COMMANDMENT OF LOVE — BROTHERLY LOVE AMONG BELIEVERS

"A new commandment I give to you, that you love one another; as I have loved you, that you also love one another.
By this all will know that you are My disciples, if you have love for one another."
—John 13:34–35, NKJV

1. The Command of Christ — Not a Suggestion

When Jesus gave His final instructions to His disciples, He did not emphasize miracles, ministries, or doctrines—He gave a commandment of love. It was not new in words, but new in measure: "As I have loved you."

This commandment is the foundation of all true Christianity.

It is the identifying mark of a disciple and the living proof of the Spirit's presence.

Without love, even truth becomes harsh, worship becomes hollow, and faith becomes lifeless.

"Though I have the gift of prophecy, and understand all mysteries and all knowledge... but have not love, I am nothing."
— 1 Corinthians 13:2, NKJV

Love is not an emotion we occasionally express; it is the very nature of God living through us. To refuse love is to resist His Spirit.

2. The Measure of Brotherly Love

Jesus defined the measure of true love:

"As I have loved you."
— John 13:34, NKJV

His love was patient with weakness, gentle with the broken, and forgiving to the undeserving. He washed the feet of the one who would betray Him and prayed for those who crucified Him.

That is the measure we are called to follow.

Brotherly love (philadelphia in Greek) means love among family—because the Church is a family, not an institution.

"Since you have purified your souls in obeying the truth through the Spirit in sincere love of the brethren, love one another fervently with a pure heart."
— 1 Peter 1:22, NKJV

Fervent love is not passive—it is active, constant, and costly. It forgives quickly, prays faithfully, and serves selflessly.

3. Love as the Mark of True Discipleship

Jesus said that the world will know His disciples by one thing—not by their preaching, their buildings, or their miracles—but by their love.

"By this all will know that you are My disciples, if you have love for one another."
— John 13:35, NKJV

Love is the greatest testimony of the Gospel.

It is the light that shines in a dark world and the fragrance that reveals Christ's presence.

When the Church walks in unity and humility, heaven touches earth.

But when love is replaced by pride, jealousy, or offense, the light grows dim and the witness fades. The world cannot see Jesus in a divided church.

4. The Consequences of Lovelessness

Jesus warned that in the last days, love would grow cold:

"And because lawlessness will abound, the love of many will grow cold."
— Matthew 24:12, NKJV

A loveless heart becomes a breeding ground for sin and deception.

Where love dies, faith weakens.

Where forgiveness is withheld, bitterness grows.

And where unity is broken, the Spirit withdraws His power.

John wrote soberly:

"He who does not love his brother abides in death."

— 1 John 3:14, NKJV

"If someone says, 'I love God,' and hates his brother, he is a liar."
— 1 John 4:20, NKJV

The absence of love is not a small flaw—it is a sign of spiritual death.

To walk in Christ is to walk in love; to forsake love is to walk away from Him.

5. Love That Forgives and Restores

The Church is not a gathering of perfect people—it is a fellowship of forgiven ones.

We all fail, but love restores.

True brotherly love covers faults, not exposes them.

"And above all things have fervent love for one another, for 'love will cover a multitude of sins.'"
— 1 Peter 4:8, NKJV

Love does not ignore truth; it heals with truth.

It confronts sin with compassion and corrects with gentleness.

A church that walks in forgiveness walks in freedom.

6. Love as Spiritual Warfare

The enemy fears a loving church more than a powerful one, because love unites what he seeks to divide.

When believers walk in love, every scheme of darkness loses ground.

Love disarms gossip, heals offenses, and silences accusation.

"Do not be overcome by evil, but overcome evil with good."
— Romans 12:21, NKJV

Every act of love is warfare.

Every word of kindness, every gesture of forgiveness, every prayer of compassion pushes back the darkness.

For where love reigns, Christ reigns.

7. Conclusion — The Law of Christ

Paul called love "the law of Christ" (Galatians 6:2, NKJV).

It fulfills every commandment and satisfies every requirement of righteousness.

Without love, holiness is incomplete; with love, the law is fulfilled.

To love your brother is to love God.

To forgive your sister is to honor the Cross.

To serve one another is to serve Christ Himself.

Love is not a feeling we choose when convenient—it is a command we obey because He first loved us.

"This is My commandment, that you love one another as I have loved you."
— John 15:12, NKJV

PRAYER AND REFLECTION

The Commandment of Love — Brotherly Love Among Believers

Reflect:

Love is not optional—it is the evidence that we belong to Christ.

Without it, our prayers lose power, our faith loses focus, and our fellowship loses life.

Christ did not say, "They will know you are My disciples by your preaching or your knowledge," but "by your love." Love is the very pulse of the Christian heart. When love ceases, the body grows cold, and the Spirit grieves.

True brotherly love is not about agreement in everything; it is about unity in the Spirit, forgiveness from the heart, and humility in relationship. The enemy knows this — which is why his greatest weapon is division. But love is stronger.

Ask yourself:

- Have I allowed offense, bitterness, or pride to quench my love for another believer?

- Have I judged when I should have forgiven, or withdrawn when I should have reconciled?

- Is there someone God is calling me to love again, even if it costs me?

Let these questions draw you to repentance and renewal, for the commandment of love is the commandment of life.

A Prayer

Heavenly Father,

You are love, and everything You do flows from love. Thank You for loving me unconditionally and for showing that love through Jesus Christ, my Lord. I acknowledge that I have not always loved others as You have loved me. Forgive me, Father, for every harsh word, unforgiven wrong, or cold heart.

Lord Jesus, You gave me a new commandment—to love as You loved. You washed the feet of the one who betrayed You and forgave those who crucified You. Teach me to love like that. Help me to walk in humility, to forgive quickly, and to seek peace with all who are Yours.

Holy Spirit, fill me anew with the love of God. Remove every trace of bitterness, pride, and division. Unite my heart with my brothers and sisters in Christ, that the world may see Your glory in our unity. Make me a vessel of grace and a messenger of reconciliation.

Let my words build up, not tear down. Let my heart remain tender. Let my love be sincere and fervent. And let Your love rule in me as the bond of perfection.

I choose today to love — freely, fully, and faithfully.

Not by feeling, but by obedience.

Not in words only, but in action and truth.

Thank You, Lord, for loving me first and calling me to walk in that same love.

In Jesus' name. Amen.

Scripture to Meditate On:

"He who does not love his brother abides in death."
— 1 John 3:14, NKJV

"By this all will know that you are My disciples, if you have love for one another."
— John 13:35, NKJV

PRAYER AND REFLECTION

The Commandment of Love — Brotherly Love Among Believers

Reflect:

Love is not optional—it is the evidence that we belong to Christ.

Without it, our prayers lose power, our faith loses focus, and our fellowship loses life.

Christ did not say, "They will know you are My disciples by your preaching or your knowledge," but "by your love." Love is the very pulse of the Christian heart. When love ceases, the body grows cold, and the Spirit grieves.

True brotherly love is not about agreement in everything; it is about unity in the Spirit, forgiveness from the heart, and humility in relationship. The enemy knows this — which is why his greatest weapon is division. But love is stronger.

Ask yourself:

- Have I allowed offense, bitterness, or pride to quench my love for another believer?

- Have I judged when I should have forgiven, or withdrawn when I should have reconciled?

- Is there someone God is calling me to love again, even if it costs me?

Let these questions draw you to repentance and renewal, for the commandment of love is the commandment of life.

A Prayer

Heavenly Father,

You are love, and everything You do flows from love. Thank You for loving me unconditionally and for showing that love through Jesus Christ, my Lord. I acknowledge that I have not always loved others as You have loved me. Forgive me, Father, for every harsh word, unforgiven wrong, or cold heart.

Lord Jesus, You gave me a new commandment—to love as You loved. You washed the feet of the one who betrayed You and forgave those who crucified You. Teach me to love like that. Help me to walk in humility, to forgive quickly, and to seek peace with all who are Yours.

Holy Spirit, fill me anew with the love of God. Remove every trace of bitterness, pride, and division. Unite my heart with my brothers and sisters in Christ, that the world may see Your glory in our unity. Make me a vessel of grace and a messenger of reconciliation.

Let my words build up, not tear down. Let my heart remain tender. Let my love be sincere and fervent. And let Your love rule in me as the bond of perfection.

I choose today to love — freely, fully, and faithfully.

Not by feeling, but by obedience.

Not in words only, but in action and truth.

Thank You, Lord, for loving me first and calling me to walk in that same love.

In Jesus' name. Amen.

Scripture to Meditate On:

"He who does not love his brother abides in death."
— 1 John 3:14, NKJV

"By this all will know that you are My disciples, if you have love for one another."
— John 13:35, NKJV

PRAYER AND REFLECTION

Love in Marriage — The Union of Christ and the Church

Reflect:

Marriage was never meant to be a struggle for control, but a story of grace.

It is not a contract built on conditions, but a covenant sealed by love — a reflection of Christ and His Bride.

Every marriage faces moments of pain, misunderstanding, and pride, but God's design was never for love to fade; it was for love to mature.

When husband and wife surrender to the Holy Spirit, love is rekindled, hearts are healed, and peace returns to the home.

Ask yourself:

- Is Christ truly the center of our marriage?

- Do I love my spouse as Christ loves me — with patience, humility, and forgiveness?

- Have I allowed pride, resentment, or neglect to quench the tenderness of our union?

Marriage is not about perfection but perseverance. It is two imperfect hearts learning daily to reflect the perfect love of God.

And when that love becomes our pursuit, the home becomes a sanctuary of His presence.

A Prayer

Heavenly Father,

Thank You for the gift of marriage — for joining two hearts, two lives, and two stories into one divine purpose. You are the author of love, and all true love begins with You.

Lord Jesus, You are the perfect Bridegroom who loved the Church and gave Yourself for her. Teach me to love with that same humility and devotion. Help me to serve, to listen, to forgive, and to honor my spouse as You have honored me with Your grace.

Holy Spirit, be the peace in our home and the voice that softens our hearts. Remove every trace of bitterness, selfishness, and pride. Let our marriage reflect the beauty of Your covenant — steadfast, sacrificial, and pure. Restore what has been broken, renew what has grown cold, and reignite the flame of love that only You can sustain.

Bless every husband to lead with gentleness and wisdom, and every wife to walk in grace and strength. Let our home be a dwelling place of Your presence — where joy reigns, prayer flows, and forgiveness abounds.

Thank You for joining us together not by chance, but by purpose.

Let our love be our worship, our unity our witness, and our faithfulness our crown.

In Jesus' name. Amen.

Scripture to Meditate On:

"Husbands, love your wives, just as Christ also loved the church and gave Himself for her."
— Ephesians 5:25, NKJV

"And now abide faith, hope, love, these three; but the greatest of these is love."
— 1 Corinthians 13:13, NKJV

CHAPTER THIRTEEN: LOVE FOR CHILDREN — THE HERITAGE OF THE LORD

"Behold, children are a heritage from the LORD, the fruit of the womb is a reward."
— Psalm 127:3, NKJV

"Train up a child in the way he should go, and when he is old he will not depart from it."
— Proverbs 22:6, NKJV

1. Children — God's Gift of Love

From the very beginning, family was born out of love.

God blessed the union of Adam and Eve with fruitfulness, saying,

"Be fruitful and multiply; fill the earth and subdue it."

— Genesis 1:28, NKJV

Children are not accidents of nature but miracles of purpose — living testimonies of divine creation.

Each child carries a piece of God's design, born for destiny and raised to reveal His image.

The psalmist calls them a heritage from the LORD — a trust, not a possession.

They belong first to God, and parents are stewards of that trust.

To raise a child in love is to partner with God in shaping eternity.

2. Love That Nurtures and Instructs

A parent's first ministry is not the pulpit or the platform — it is the home.

Children learn who God is not by sermons, but by example.

Every word, every tone, every prayer becomes a lesson written on their hearts.

"And these words which I command you today shall be in your heart. You shall teach them diligently to your children..."
— Deuteronomy 6:6–7, NKJV

True love disciplines, but never destroys.

It corrects with compassion and guides with patience.

Love teaches by modeling integrity, humility, and faith.

Children who grow up seeing prayer in the home will one day pray on their own.

They will carry the faith they first saw lived before them.

3. The Father's Example and the Mother's Influence

Fathers and mothers are the first reflection of God that children see.

A father reveals God's strength and guidance.

A mother reflects His tenderness and compassion.

"As a father pities his children, so the LORD pities those who fear Him."
— Psalm 103:13, NKJV

"She watches over the ways of her household, and does not eat the bread of idleness."
— Proverbs 31:27, NKJV

When a father leads with love and integrity, his children feel secure.

When a mother nurtures with gentleness and wisdom, her children flourish.

Together, they form a picture of the Father's perfect balance of truth and grace.

Even when parents fall short, God's mercy covers their weakness — for His love fills the gaps we cannot.

4. Love That Disciplines with Grace

The world teaches indulgence; God teaches discipline.

True love does not spoil — it shapes.

It understands that correction is not rejection but redirection.

"For whom the LORD loves He corrects, just as a father the son in whom he delights."
— Proverbs 3:12, NKJV

Discipline without love produces rebellion.

Love without discipline produces ruin.

But discipline wrapped in love produces wisdom and strength.

Every act of correction, when done in love, points the child back to the heart of God — a Father who disciplines not to harm, but to heal.

5. Love That Blesses and Prays

One of the greatest legacies a parent can leave is the power of a blessing.

Throughout Scripture, godly parents spoke blessings over their children — releasing destiny, identity, and divine favor.

"The LORD bless you and keep you; the LORD make His face shine upon you..."
— Numbers 6:24–25, NKJV

Parents are called not only to provide but to pray — to stand as spiritual covering over their children.

Every whispered prayer shapes their future. Every word of blessing opens a door of grace.

Love that prays never ceases.

Even when children wander, a parent's prayers can bring them home.

6. The Warning — The Cost of Loveless Parenting

The absence of love in a home is more destructive than poverty or hardship.

A child starved of affection grows empty in spirit.

A home without love breeds wounds that only God can heal.

"And you, fathers, do not provoke your children to wrath, but bring them up in the training and admonition of the Lord."
— Ephesians 6:4, NKJV

Harsh words, neglect, or favoritism can wound deeply.

But grace can restore what has been broken.

Where love has failed, repentance can rebuild.

God specializes in restoring families, renewing hearts, and healing generations.

7. The Legacy of Love

Every child raised in love becomes a carrier of that same love to others.

The greatest inheritance we can give our children is not wealth, but faith.

Faith that knows God's voice. Faith that trusts His Word. Faith that walks in His love.

"But as for me and my house, we will serve the LORD."
— Joshua 24:15, NKJV

A home ruled by love becomes a lighthouse in a dark world — a place where Christ is seen, known, and adored.

Such a home leaves a legacy that outlives its walls.

8. Conclusion — The Father's Heart in the Home

The home is the first church, and parents are its shepherds.

To raise children in love is to reflect the Father's own heart — patient, merciful, and steadfast.

In the end, the greatest success of a parent is not measured in worldly achievement but in the echo of these words in heaven:

"They knew Me through your love."

"I have no greater joy than to hear that my children walk in truth."
— 3 John 1:4, NKJV

PRAYER AND REFLECTION

Love for Children — The Heritage of the Lord

Reflect:

Every child born is a message from God that the world must continue.

Children are not given to us merely to raise — they are entrusted to us to reflect God's love.

Parenthood is holy ground.

It is in the home that the first prayers are heard, the first acts of forgiveness are taught, and the first glimpses of God's character are seen.

When parents love as God loves — with patience, consistency, and grace — children learn to trust, to forgive, and to believe.

But when love fades, confusion grows.

A loveless home creates generations who do not know the heart of the Father.

Ask yourself:

- Have I raised or treated my children in the love and fear of the Lord?

- Have I spoken words that heal, or words that wound?

- Do I pray for my children's hearts as much as their future?

- Have I reflected the Father's heart within my home?

Let the Holy Spirit remind you that it is never too late to begin again.

God can restore love where there has been pain and renew faith where there has been fear.

A Prayer

Heavenly Father,

Thank You for the precious gift of children — the heritage of Your love and the reflection of Your heart. You have entrusted them to us, not as possessions, but as souls to be nurtured, taught, and guided in Your ways.

Lord Jesus, You welcomed little children into Your arms and blessed them. Help me to see them as You do — pure, valuable, and full of divine purpose. Teach me to love them with patience, to discipline with wisdom, and to lead them by example in righteousness and truth.

Holy Spirit, dwell in our home. Let Your peace rule in every room, Your presence fill every heart, and Your Word shape every conversation. Heal every place where love has been broken. Restore unity between parents and children, and cause Your grace to rebuild the walls that sin and hurt have torn down.

Bless every father to lead with compassion, every mother to nurture with tenderness, and every child to walk in obedience and honor. Let our home be a sanctuary of love — where laughter, prayer, and truth abide.

And for every parent who has failed or feels unworthy, remind them that Your mercy is greater. You are the God who redeems time and restores generations.

Thank You, Father, for Your unfailing love.

May my family reflect Your kingdom on earth — rooted in love, walking in truth, and shining with Your glory.

In Jesus' name. Amen.

Scripture to Meditate On:

*"And these words which I command you today shall be in your heart.
You shall teach them diligently to your children..."*
— Deuteronomy 6:6–7, NKJV

"I have no greater joy than to hear that my children walk in truth."
— 3 John 1:4, NKJV

CHAPTER FOURTEEN: THE LOVE OF GOD'S CHILDREN FOR THE FATHER

"You shall love the LORD your God with all your heart, with all your soul, and with all your mind."
— Matthew 22:37, NKJV

"We love Him because He first loved us."
— 1 John 4:19, NKJV

1. Love Returning to Its Source

Love began in God, flowed through Christ, and now calls His children to return it.

Every expression of love — brotherly, marital, parental — finds its perfection when it leads us back to the Father Himself.

The greatest commandment in all of Scripture is not about what we do for God but about how we love Him.

"And now, Israel, what does the LORD your God require of you, but to fear the LORD your God, to walk in all His ways and to love Him…"
— Deuteronomy 10:12, NKJV

The Father's love is not casual; it is covenantal.

He calls His children not only to believe, but to belong — not only to serve, but to love.

Our relationship with God is not built on fear of punishment but on gratitude for redemption.

We love Him because He first loved us.

2. The Heart, Soul, and Mind of Love

Jesus summarized the law and the prophets in one simple yet infinite command:

"You shall love the LORD your God with all your heart, with all your soul, and with all your mind."
— Matthew 22:37, NKJV

This is total love — love that engages the heart (our emotions), the soul (our will and devotion), and the mind (our thoughts and understanding).

Loving God is not a moment of worship but a manner of life.

It means seeking Him in every choice, preferring Him above all desires, and aligning every thought with His truth.

To love God with all your heart is to give Him your affection.

To love Him with all your soul is to surrender your will.

To love Him with all your mind is to devote your understanding to His Word.

This is not religion; it is relationship — love expressed in every breath.

3. Love Proven in Obedience

Love for God cannot be separated from obedience to His Word.

Jesus made it unmistakably clear:

"If you love Me, keep My commandments."
— John 14:15, NKJV

Obedience is the language of love.

It is not the cold performance of duty, but the warm response of a grateful heart.

A child who truly loves the Father will not obey out of fear, but out of devotion.

When love is the motive, obedience becomes joy.

"For this is the love of God, that we keep His commandments. And His commandments are not burdensome."
— 1 John 5:3, NKJV

Every time we choose His will over ours, we say, "Father, I love You."

4. Love That Worships and Delights

The truest love for God is not only expressed in obedience but in adoration.

Love delights to be in His presence, to hear His voice, and to behold His beauty.

*"Whom have I in heaven but You? And there is none upon earth that
I desire besides You."*
— Psalm 73:25, NKJV

Worship is not merely a song — it is the overflow of love.

It is the heart bowing before its Source, saying, "Abba, Father."

The Father seeks such worshipers — not those who perform, but those who pursue; not those who impress, but those who love.

"But the hour is coming, and now is, when the true worshipers will worship the Father in spirit and truth; for the Father is seeking such to worship Him."
— John 4:23, NKJV

When love fills worship, heaven touches earth.

5. The Reward of Loving the Father

To love God is to walk in continual fellowship with Him.

Love opens heaven's secrets and draws the soul into divine intimacy.

"He who has My commandments and keeps them, it is he who loves Me. And he who loves Me will be loved by My Father, and I will love him and manifest Myself to him."
— John 14:21, NKJV

Love for God does not go unanswered.

The Father reveals Himself more deeply to those who seek Him in love.

He becomes not just Lord, but Friend — not just Creator, but Father.

When we love Him, fear fades, joy grows, and peace becomes constant.

Love perfects faith and makes obedience beautiful.

6. The Danger of Forsaking Love

Jesus warned the Church of Ephesus with sobering words:

"Nevertheless I have this against you, that you have left your first love."
— Revelation 2:4, NKJV

They had works, labor, and endurance — but they had lost intimacy.

They were busy for God but distant from God.

When love fades, devotion becomes duty, prayer becomes performance, and worship becomes noise.

A heart that ceases to love becomes a heart that soon forgets.

The remedy Jesus gave was simple:

"Remember... repent... and do the first works."
— Revelation 2:5, NKJV

Return to the place of love — the altar of the heart, where gratitude burns and the Father's presence dwells.

7. The Eternal Fellowship of Love

The greatest joy of heaven will not be the streets of gold or the gates of pearl, but the presence of the Father.

To see Him face to face — the One we loved in faith — will be the final reward of every child of God.

"And I will be a Father to you, and you shall be My sons and daughters, says the LORD Almighty."
— 2 Corinthians 6:18, NKJV

In eternity, love will no longer be hindered by flesh or fear.

It will be perfect, unbroken, everlasting.

The children will dwell forever in the arms of the Father who loved them before the world began.

8. Conclusion — Love's Full Circle

Love began in the Father's heart.

It was revealed through the Son, poured out by the Spirit, and perfected in the hearts of His children.

Now it returns to where it came from — to the Father, whose essence is Love Himself.

To love God is not just the greatest commandment — it is the highest privilege.

It is what we were created for, redeemed for, and destined for.

And when we love Him with all our heart, soul, and mind, the circle of love is complete.

"And this is eternal life, that they may know You, the only true God, and Jesus Christ whom You have sent."
— John 17:3, NKJV

PRAYER AND REFLECTION

The Love of God's Children for the Father

Reflect:

All creation began with love, and all redemption ends with love returning to the Father.

We were not created first to serve, or to strive — but to love Him.

It is the greatest commandment, and yet the simplest:

"You shall love the LORD your God with all your heart, with all your soul, and with all your mind."

This is the heartbeat of every true believer.

To love God is to delight in His presence, to obey His Word, to trust His will, and to treasure His nearness above all else.

When we love Him, obedience is no longer a burden — it becomes our joy.

When we love Him, worship is not a duty — it becomes our breath.

When we love Him, fear disappears — for perfect love casts out fear.

Ask yourself:

- Do I love the Father with my whole heart — above every desire, dream, and distraction?

- Have I allowed the cares of this world to cool my affection for Him?

- Do I still delight in His presence as I once did?

Let the Holy Spirit rekindle your first love — the flame that once burned only for Him.

For this is the mystery of love fulfilled: that what began in the heart of God returns to Him in the hearts of His children.

A Prayer

Heavenly Father,

You are Love itself — eternal, unchanging, and pure. From Your heart came life, and through

Your mercy came redemption. Thank You for loving me first, even when I was unworthy. Thank You for calling me Your child, for forgiving my sins, and for drawing me into Your presence.

Lord Jesus, You revealed the Father's love in human form. You showed me how to walk in obedience, to trust in every trial, and to worship in spirit and truth. You gave all for love, and through Your sacrifice, I have been brought near.

Holy Spirit, fill my heart again with holy affection for the Father. Remove every distraction, every idol, every fear that competes for my love. Teach me to love the Lord with all my heart, all my soul, and all my mind. Let my life be a continual song of devotion.

Father, I give You all that I am — my thoughts, my will, my time, and my future.

Let my obedience be my worship. Let my words reflect Your truth. Let my heart remain steadfast in love until the day I see You face to face.

I love You, Father — not for what You give, but for who You are.

You are my beginning and my end, my portion forever.

May my life bring You glory, and may my love for You never fade.

In Jesus' name. Amen.

Scripture to Meditate On:

"If you love Me, keep My commandments."
— John 14:15, NKJV

"Whom have I in heaven but You? And there is none upon earth that I desire besides You."
— Psalm 73:25, NKJV

"We love Him because He first loved us."
— 1 John 4:19, NKJV

EPILOGUE:
THE MYSTERY COMPLETE
— LOVE RETURNING
HOME

Before the first star was set in the heavens, before time began its count, there was Love.

Love spoke light into existence.

Love formed humanity from the dust.

Love walked in the garden, calling out, "Where are you?"

And though man turned away, Love pursued.

Through covenants and prophets, through promise and patience, Love never stopped reaching.

In the fullness of time, Love put on flesh.

He came not crowned in gold, but wrapped in swaddling cloth.

He healed the broken, embraced the rejected, and carried the cross of our redemption.

Love obeyed — even unto death.

Then, from the tomb, Love rose again.

He poured out His Spirit, filling hearts with divine fire,

turning fear into faith, and faith into fellowship.

From there, Love continued its journey — flowing into marriages, into families, into churches, into nations.

Wherever Love lives, heaven touches earth.

But Love's story is not complete until it returns to its Source.

Every prayer whispered in faith, every act of mercy, every tear of repentance rises like incense to the throne of the Father.

For from Him, through Him, and to Him are all things — and Love is the circle that never ends.

The Father loved us into being.

The Son loved us into redemption.

The Spirit loves us into transformation.

And we, His children, are called to love Him back into eternity.

This is the Mystery of Love — that the infinite God chose to share His heart, to make Himself known, and to dwell forever with those who love Him. When all things fade and every kingdom falls, only Love will remain.

"And now abide faith, hope, love, these three; but the greatest of these is love."
— 1 Corinthians 13:13, NKJV

ACKNOWLEDGMENTS

All glory, honor, and praise belong to the Lord God Almighty, who is Love Himself — the Author, the Giver, and the Fulfillment of all that is good.

Without His presence, grace, and revelation, this book would not exist.

I bow my heart before the Father, who revealed His unfathomable love from eternity; to the Son, Jesus Christ, the visible expression of that love upon the cross; and to the Holy Spirit, who continues to pour the Father's love into my heart, guiding every word and thought within these pages

To those who long to understand the love of God — this book was written for you.

May every word draw you closer to the One who calls you beloved.

And finally, to the readers who open these pages:

Thank you for allowing me to share my heart with you.

May The Mystery of Love awaken your spirit to the beauty, depth, and eternity of God's love — until that day when we stand before Him, where love is no longer spoken, but fully known.

"The LORD has appeared of old to me, saying:
'Yes, I have loved you with an everlasting love;
Therefore with lovingkindness I have drawn you.'"
— Jeremiah 31:3, NKJV

FINAL PRAYER

The Song of Love Returned

Heavenly Father,

The story of love began in You.

Before there was breath, before there was light, there was Your heart — a heart overflowing with mercy, grace, and goodness.

You loved the world into being, and when the world turned away, You loved it back into redemption.

From the dust of Eden to the Cross of Calvary, Your love has never failed and never faded.

Thank You, Father, for revealing to me the mystery of Your love — the love that forgives the sinner, restores the broken, and calls the lost home.

Lord Jesus, You are Love made flesh — the Word who walked among us, the Lamb who took away our sin, and the Bridegroom who still calls,

"Come to Me." You obeyed the Father's will, endured the cross, and opened the way for us to know Love Himself.

Holy Spirit, You are the fire of divine affection burning within us.

You teach, convict, and comfort.

You pour the Father's love into our hearts until it overflows. Fill me continually with that love — to love God with all my heart, soul, and mind, and to love others as Christ has loved me.

Lord, let my life be a vessel of Your love. Let my words bring healing, my hands serve others, and my heart stay tender before You.

When I am tested, refine my love.

When I am weary, renew it.

When I am wounded, restore it.

And when my journey on this earth is done, let the final word on my lips be the same as Yours — Love.

For You alone are my beginning, my purpose, and my end.

May every reader who opens these pages encounter not my words, but Your heart, O God — the endless mystery, the unsearchable depth, the everlasting truth:

You are Love.

I give You all the glory, forever and ever.

In Jesus' name. Amen.

Scripture to Rest Upon:

"We love Him because He first loved us."
— 1 John 4:19, NKJV

"The grace of our Lord Jesus Christ, and the love of God, and the communion of the Holy Spirit be with you all. Amen."
— 2 Corinthians 13:14, NKJV